THE HIGH CROSSES
OF IRELAND

EARLY CHRISTIAN SYMBOLISM
IN GREAT BRITAIN AND IRELAND

THE
HIGH
CROSSES
OF
IRELAND

J Romilly
ALLEN

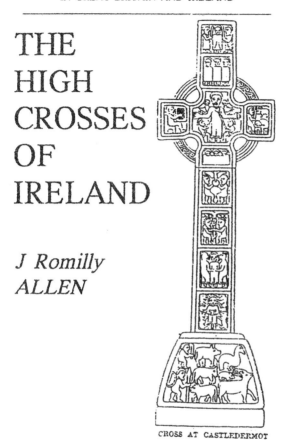

CROSS AT CASTLEDERMOT

ISBN 0947992 90 1
Facsimile reprint 1992
by Llanerch Publishers,
Felinfach. First published
in 1887 by Whiting & Co., London.

Other Llanerch titles include:

SYMBOLISM OF THE CELTIC CROSS
by Derek Bryce

TALIESIN POEMS
translated by Meirion Pennar

NORTHUMBRIAN CROSSES
by W. G. Collingwood

MABINOGION: THE FOUR BRANCHES
the Guest translation

CELTIC FOLK-TALES
by F. M. Luzel..

For a complete list, write to Llanerch Publishers,
Felinfach, Lampeter, Dyfed, Wales, SA48 8PJ.

Publisher's note: only the contents, indices,
and list of illustrations have been repaginated;
the main part of the text retains the original
page numbers.

CONTENTS

LECTURE III.

THE HIGH CROSSES OF IRELAND.

TENTH CENTURY.

IN studying the history of Christian art it will be noticed that each period is characterised by particular doctrines which attained special prominence at the time, and were therefore chosen in preference to all others as the subjects most suitable for illustration. Each new generation also looked upon the same doctrine from an entirely new point of view, and gave fresh interpretations of the various texts of Scripture upon which it was founded. Thus, during the first three centuries of the Christian era, we find no representations whatever of our Lord's Passion, whereas in later times the Crucifixion is the commonest subject of all.

The early Church looked upon the death of Christ only as a means to an end, that end being the Redemption of the world. This is clearly shown by the pictures of Daniel in the Den of Lions, and the other series of symbolical paintings in the Catacombs, which express faith in the power of God to save the sinner through the blood of Christ. The mediæval mind, however, dwelt almost entirely on the bodily suffering of the Saviour, to the exclusion of the objects for which the pain was endured.

Besides the changes in the subjects chosen for illustration in Christian art, due to difference of time, we have also to consider the alterations produced by planting Christianity in a new geographical area. Thus, in the Catacombs there are no pictures of the Devil, except where he appears as the Serpent tempting Adam and Eve; but as soon as the Northern nations were incorporated in Christendom, the effect of the Teutonic imagination becomes at once apparent in the revolting conceptions of the tortures of the damned, which owe their origin chiefly to pagan mythology.

Not only has each period in the history of Christian art its special set of subjects, but the varying conditions of ecclesiastical life, as regards the wealth and position of the Church in different countries, produced corresponding changes in the monuments and objects upon which the symbolism manifests itself. The natural materials available for construction in each country, and the aptitude of particular races for the arts of painting, sculpture, or metal-work, are also considerations which must not be neglected. For instance, during the first three centuries the persecution of the Church by the State caused all Christian art to be confined to the hidden recesses of the underground cemeteries ; and the danger attending the occupation of the sculptor, in case his religious opinions should become known, made painting a safer and easier method of decoration. When the persecutions ceased sculpture was applied to the decoration of sarcophagi, and with the building of the first basilicas above-ground the era of mosaics commenced.

From the time when Charlemagne revived literary learning in the eighth century, the art of illuminating manuscripts with miniatures illustrating the Scriptures, etc., was extensively practised. After the Classical School of sculpture died out, with discontinuance of making elaborate sarcophagi for the reception of the dead, a new school arose in Lombardy, who used sculpture largely in the decorative features of their churches. In Great Britain Christian art was so far modified, first in Ireland and then in Scotland, as to constitute a national style, differing essentially from any other, both in its ornamental features and its symbolism. When the Church became rich, after the eleventh century, ecclesiastical buildings were most lavishly ornamented in every way, with painting, sculpture, stained glass, and carved woodwork ; and the metal-worker, the enameller, and the jeweller, vied with each other in beautifying the shrines of saints and the vessels used for performing the sacred rites.

It appears, then, in dealing with the history of early Christian symbolism, that there are three factors to be taken into account:—1. The class of monuments or objects upon which the symbolism chiefly occurs. 2. The special set of subjects characteristic of the period. 3. The particular treatment of subjects peculiar to the time and country.

In the present lecture we are concerned with the ninth, tenth, and eleventh centuries, which may be called the period of the sculptured crosses, as it is from these monuments that our knowledge of the condition of early Christian art in Great Britain is principally derived.

We shall now proceed to examine the symbolism of the crosses in detail, with a view to determining the subjects most frequently represented and the special methods of treatment adopted.

The crosses in question are found in connection with ecclesiastical buildings in England, Wales, Scotland, and Ireland, and although possessing certain features in common, such as interlacing and other forms of ornament, yet each group has its distinct local characteristics, which will be described in due course. The object of the erection of the more important free standing crosses was not as sepulchral memorials, but they were intended to be either dedicatory, commemorative, terminal, churchyard, or wayside crosses, being always placed in a prominent position, so as to attract the attention of the passer-by, and direct his mind to the contemplation of holy things, and more especially the Crucifixion and Resurrection of our Lord.

We have seen, in the last lecture, that the symbolism of the purely sepulchral monument was confined almost entirely to the cross and monograms of the name of Christ, but the erect crosses are covered with the most elaborate sculptures, representing scenes from Scripture and other subjects. The object in the former case was to mark the resting-place of the deceased, and to express, in the simplest manner possible, the hope of a future life in Christ; whereas in the latter the chief aim was to set forth the leading doctrines of Christianity, by means of outward forms, for the instruction of the unlearned, and to excite feelings of devotion and reverence in the minds of all persons visiting the sacred precincts. Thus, the cross of Fland at Clonmacnois, when referred to in the *Annals of the Four*

Masters, is called either the "High Cross" (under the year A.D. 957) or the "Cross of the Scriptures" (under the year A.D. 1060).[1] The inscriptions upon the high crosses of Ireland show that these monuments were not sepulchral, because in cases where names of persons are mentioned they are known to have been buried elsewhere.

The cross in Kells churchyard is inscribed, "Patricii et Columbæ Crux" (the Cross of SS. Patrick and Columba); and since neither of the saints here mentioned were buried at Kells, and the character of the ornamentation of the cross showing it to belong to the ninth century, it is clear that the monument is commemorative. We have seen examples of dedicatory inscriptions to St. Peter upon early pillar-stones at Kilnasaggart, in the county of Armagh, and at Whithorne in Wigtonshire; and Fordun relates that in the year A.D. 1260 a cross of great magnificence was dug up at Peebles, upon the base of which was the inscription, "Locus Sancti Nicholai Episcopi".[2]

Many of the high crosses appear to have been terminal, marking the limits of the sanctuary,—as, for instance, at Castle Kieran, co. Meath, the eight mile-crosses at Ripon in Yorkshire,[3] and four at Hexham in Northumberland. Most of the early crosses in Cornwall are situated near the principal doorways of churches, so as to command the attention of worshippers entering the sacred edifice.

The general character of the symbolism of the high crosses of Ireland will be best understood from a description of some of the more important examples. There are at present remaining in Ireland about thirty high crosses,[4] in more or less perfect condition, out of which six have inscriptions by which their dates have been fixed,[5] and two others have inscriptions giving no clue to their age.[6]

The ordinary parish churches in Ireland do not differ much

---

[1] Petrie's *Irish Inscr.*, vol. i, p. 43.

[2] *Forduni Scotichron.*, vol. ii, p. 96 ; quoted in Stuart's *Sculptured Stones*, vol. ii, p. 53.

[3] Walbran's *Guide to Ripon*, p. 30.

[4] O'Neill's *Ancient Crosses of Ireland;* Petrie's *Irish Inscr.*, vol. ii, p. 153.

[5] At Clonmacnois, Monasterboice. Cong (2), and Tuam (2).

[6] At Delgany and Kells.

from those in other parts of Great Britain, except that they are generally smaller and simpler in ground-plan; but on the more celebrated ecclesiastical sites we find groups of buildings quite unlike anything to be seen elsewhere, consisting of an isolated round tower, several small churches, and one or more free standing crosses. The most remarkable examples are at Clonmacnois, King's County; Monasterboice, co. Louth; and Kells, co. Meath.

Others with figure-sculpture exist at Donaghmore and Ardboe, co. Tyrone; Tynan and Armagh, co. Armagh; Clones, co. Monaghan; Drumcliff, co. Sligo; Tuam, co. Galway; Termonfeckin, co. Louth; St. Kieran's, co. Meath; Durrow, King's County; Kilcullen, Castle Dermot, and Moone Abbey, co. Kildare; Ullard, Graigne na managh, Killamery, and Kilklispeen, co. Kilkenny. Readers desirous of obtaining a fuller knowledge of Irish ecclesiastical architecture are referred to the works on the subject by Lord Dunraven, Miss Margaret Stokes, Petrie, Wakeman, and Marcus Keane; also to Dr. J. Anderson's *Scotland in Early Christian Times*, 1st Series.

CROSSES AT MONASTERBOICE.

Monasterboice is situated in the county of Louth, six miles north-west of the town of Drogheda. The name is derived from Mainister Buiti, which means the Monastery of Buite, or Boetius, an Irish bishop, whose death is recorded in the *Annals of the Four Masters* as having taken place on the 7th December, A.D. 521. The remains existing at present are of much later date, and consist of a round tower, 110 ft. high, two small churches, and three elaborately sculptured crosses. Two of these crosses stand in their original positions, in a more or less perfect state of preservation; but the third has been broken, and the head and part of the shaft which remain have been re-erected in the old socket-stone.

The largest of the two perfect crosses is 22 ft. high (including the base, which is 1 ft. 6 ins. high), and is situated on the south side of the church nearest the round tower. It is called the Great Cross of Monasterboice. The other is 19 ft. high (including the base, which is 2 ft. 3 ins. high), and stands at the south-east corner of the church farthest from the round tower.

It is called the Cross of Muiredach,[1] from the abbot of that name, by whom the monument was erected.   It is the most beautiful specimen of Celtic stonework now in existence, and the date is known from the inscription.   We will, therefore, examine this cross first, as a typical example with which the others may be compared.   It is composed of three separate stones, joined together by mortices and tenons, the base or socket forming the first, the shaft and two horizontal arms making the second, and the top arm of the cross being the third.   The base is in the shape of a truncated pyramid of four sides, measuring 2 ft. 2 ins. high, 4 ft. 9 ins. at the bottom, tapering to 3 ft. 8 ins. by 3 ft. 4 ins. at the top.   The shaft is rectangular, 6 ft. 6 ins. high, 2 ft. 6 ins. by 1 ft. 8 ins. at the bottom, tapering to 2 ft. 4 ins. by 1 ft. 7 ins. at the top.   The form of the cross is that described in the last lecture (fig. 17, No. 4) as being typically Celtic, with four semicircular hollows in the angles, made by the inter- section of the arms, and having a connecting circular ring.   The Irish crosses differ from those of Scotland, for, instead of having the cross sculptured in relief upon an upright slab, the whole stone is cut out into the shape of the cross, with the hollows be- tween the encircling ring and the arms pierced right through. The effect of the outline of the cross standing out against the sky is far more beautiful than the appearance of the Scotch slabs. In the middle of each of the four semicircular hollows are little round projections, which emphasise the whole and take away from the effect of weakness produced by the hollows.   The top stone is in the shape of a little house, with a sloping roof like the metal shrines of the period, and has a crescent-shaped finial at each end.[2]   A bead or roll moulding runs round all the edges of the cross, and the sculpture is arranged in rectangular panels, each enclosed within a frame of cable moulding.   The cross is made of a yellowish sandstone.

On the west face, at the bottom of the shaft, is an Irish inscription in minuscules—

[1] O'Neill calls it the south-east cross, from its position with regard to the round tower.

[2] Some crosses, like those at Kilklispeen, co. Kilkenny, are surmounted by a conical stone.   See representation of the Temple, in the scene of the "Temptation of Christ", in the *Book of Kells*.   (Westwood's *Miniatures*, pl. 11.)

OR̄ DO MUIREDACH LAS (A)NDERNAD IN CHRO(SS)A

("Pray for Muiredach, by whom this cross was made."[1]) The
deaths of two persons of the name of Muiredach, who were connected with Monasterboice, are recorded by the *Four Masters*:
"A.D. 844. Muredach, son of Flann, Abbot of Mainister Buite,
died." "A.D. 923 or 924. Muiredach, son of Domhnall, tanist
Abbot of Armagh, and chief steward of the southern Hy Neill,
and successor of Buite, the son of Branach, head of the council
of all the men of Bregia, laity and clergy, departed this life on
the 5th day of the calends of December." The inscription probably refers to the latter, since he was the most important per-
sonage of the two, and therefore more likely to have been the
erector of a monument of such celebrity, and also because the
style of the sculptures corresponds so nearly with those on the
cross of King Fland at Clonmacnois, which was set up between
the years A.D. 914 and 924.

The general scheme of the decoration and symbolism of all
the Irish high crosses is more or less the same. The leading
feature is always the Crucifixion, which occupies the centre of
the head on the front cross, whilst Christ in Glory is placed in
a corresponding position on the back. The spaces on the arms
are filled in with the accessories of the central subjects. Upon
the shaft are a series of scenes from Scripture, leading the mind
on to the main doctrine of the Christian faith. The sides and
other portions of the cross are ornamented with alternate panels
of geometrical patterns of the usual Celtic type, and miscel-
laneous figure-subjects. The base, or socket-stone, is usually
sculptured with symbolical subjects, more nearly resembling
those found upon the upright cross-slabs of the east of Scotland
than any of the rest of the design. The scenes portrayed consist of ecclesiastics, men in chariots, warriors, huntsmen, animals,
and fabulous beasts, such as centaurs.

The figure-subjects sculptured upon the cross of Muiredach,
at Monasterboice, are as follows:—

On the front.—On the centre of the head of the cross is the
Crucifixion, with the soldiers bearing the spear and sponge.
Beneath the feet of the Saviour is a bird, and on each side of

[1] Petrie's *Irish Inscriptions*, vol. ii, p. 66.

His head an angel. A kneeling figure and an angel are place near the soldiers to fill up the space.

On the right arm is a group of six figures and an animal; on the left arm a group of six figures holding musical instruments or other objects; and on the top arm a figure with both hands upraised, and another figure on each side.

On the shaft are three panels, each containing a group of three figures, wearing elaborately ornamented vestments reaching down nearly to the feet. The sculpture on the top panel represents an enthroned figure in the centre, delivering a book and a staff to figures standing on either side. The next panel shows three standing figures, probably of saints or ecclesiastics, holding books, the central one being in the act of giving the benediction. The group in the bottom panel consists of a central figure, being led away by two soldiers armed with swords, and is supposed to be intended for Christ seized by the Jews. Nearly all the figures have heavy moustachios and thick curling hair. The nimbus is entirely absent. The inscription is on this face at the bottom of the shaft, and in front of it are carved two cat-like animals in high relief, one holding a bird and the other a toad (?) between its claws. On the base are sculptures of animals almost entirely defaced.

On the back.—On the head and arms of the cross is a group of more than forty-five figures, representing the scene of the Last Judgment. In the centre Christ standing up and holding a floriated sceptre in the right hand and the Cross of the Resurrection in the left. Resting on the head of our Lord is a bird, perhaps intended for the Phœnix, the symbol of the Resurrection. At the feet of the Saviour is a small kneeling figure with an open book above the head. On the right is David enthroned, playing the harp, upon which the Holy Spirit rests in the form of a dove, to symbolise the inspiration of the Psalmist; and further on behind are the choir of angels playing trumpets. On the left are the lost souls, being driven away from the presence of Christ by a fiend holding a trident; below the figure of the Saviour is the Archangel Michael weighing the souls, and above a soul being carried to heaven by two angels (?). On the top arm of the cross are two ecclesiastics with croziers, placed crosswise, and a circular disc between them. On the shaft are four panels with groups of figures, the top one representing the Adoration of the Magi, and the bottom one the Temptation and Expulsion of Adam and Eve. The subjects on the two middle panels have not yet been explained. At the bottom of the shaft are a pair of animals carved in high relief. On the base are sculptures of animals almost entirely defaced.

On the right side.—On the top arm of the cross is a figure on horseback ; on the end of the side arm, Pilate washing his hands ; underneath the side arm, two animals ; and on the edge of the circular ring, pairs of twisted serpents with human heads between each twist. At the bottom of the shaft are a pair of animals carved in high relief. On the base the sculpture is defaced.

On the left side.—On the top arm are two ecclesiastics, with croziers placed crosswise, and a bird, holding a circular disc in its beak, between them ; on the end of the side arm, Christ, with a bird resting on His head, led away by the Jews to Caiaphas ; and underneath the side arm, the Hand Symbol, or Dextera Dei.

At the bottom of the shaft are two figures, carved in high relief, representing men with long hair and heavy moustachios, grasping each other's beards.

On the base is a man on horseback, preceded by a satyr, holding a trident, and a centaur shooting with a bow and arrow. We will now proceed to discuss the subjects of the sculpture.

The Crucifixion.—Representations of the sufferings of our Lord upon the cross do not occur amongst the paintings in the Catacombs of Rome during the first four centuries. This entire omission of scenes from the Passion from the cycle of subjects chosen for illustration in early Christian art may be accounted for partly by the repulsion with which the first converts from paganism looked upon crucifixion as a mode of death. Another reason for not openly displaying pictures of the sufferings of Our Lord, was in order to avoid the ridicule which the idea of a crucified God seems to have excited in the minds of unbelievers. Curiously enough, one of the most ancient representations of the Crucifixion is a blasphemous caricature scratched in outline with a pointed instrument upon the plaster walls of the palace of the Cæsars on the Palatine Hill at Rome.[1] It was discovered in 1857, and is now preserved in the Kircherian Museum at Rome. The sketch or "graffito" shows a man with the head of an ass, attached to a cross, at the foot of which stands a Christian. The meaning of the caricature is explained by the inscription in Greek, "Alexamenos worships God".

The method of representing the Crucifixion at the present time has been arrived at by a gradual process of development, as has been the case with most other Christian symbols. In the previous lecture the evolution of the cross out of the Chi-Rho monogram was explained; we shall now show how the Crucifixion was the outcome of a combination of the Lamb of God and the cross.

On the sculptured sarcophagi at Rome and elsewhere, of the fifth and sixth centuries, the Agnus Dei is seen bearing the Chi-Rho monogram on its forehead, then with the plain cross on the forehead, then carrying a cross on its shoulder, then placed on an altar with a cross behind it, and showing wounds with blood flowing; and lastly, the Lamb is enclosed within a medallion forming the centre of a cross.[2] A unique instance of the Agnus Dei upon the cross occurs on a sculptured slab in Wirksworth Church, Derbyshire, which will be described subsequently. The next step was to substitute the actual figure of the Saviour for the symbolical Lamb. This change was effected by the Quinisext Council, held at Constantinople in A.D. 683, which decreed as follows: " We pronounce that the form of Him who taketh away the sin of the world, the Lamb of Christ our Lord, be set up in human shape on images henceforth, instead of the Lamb, formerly used."[3]

Scenes from the Passion only occur on one of the sculptured sarcophagi in the Lateran Museum at Rome,[4] and the Cruci-

---

[1] Martigny's *Dict.*, art. " Calomnies", p. 110.

[2] As on the bronze station-cross at Mayence (St. John Tyrwhitt's *Art Teaching of the Primitive Church*, p. 249); and on the ivory cross of King Ferdinand (A.D. 1063) in the Madrid Museum (J. F. Riaño, *Industrial Arts in Spain*, p. 137). The earliest instance is on the Vatican Cross presented by Justin II to Rome in the sixth century (Martigny's *Dict.*, p. 226).

[3] St. J. Tyrwhitt's *Art Teaching of the Primitive Church*, p. 240.

[4] Appell's *Monuments of Early Christian Art*, p. 21.

fixion is not included in the series. A very early instance of
the Crucifixion amongst the scenes from the Passion is to be
found on a set of four ivory plaques in the British Museum,[1]

Fig. 31.—Early Sculptured Slab at Wirksworth.

which are executed in the same style of art as the sculptured
sarcophagi of the sixth century at Rome.

Probably the earliest illuminated MS. containing a miniature

---

[1] Westwood's *Catal. of Fictile Ivories,* p. 44.

of the Crucifixion, with the actual figure of Christ in place of the Lamb, is the celebrated Syriac copy of the Four Gospels in the Medici-Laurentian Library at Florence, which was written in the year 586, by Rabula, a scribe, in the monastery of St. John, in Zagby, a city of Mesopotamia.[1] Here Christ is shown crucified with the two thieves; above are the sun and moon, and on each side below the soldier piercing our Lord's right side with a spear (his name, LONGINOS, being inscribed over his head), and the sponge-bearer carrying a vessel with vinegar. The other figures in the scene are three soldiers seated on the ground, casting lots for the garments, in the centre; the Virgin Mary and St. John on the left side of the picture, and three other women on the right. The heads of Christ and the Virgin Mary only are surrounded by the nimbus. The arms and feet of the Saviour are bare, but the rest of the body is clothed in a loose tunic. Life has not yet become extinct, for the eyes are open. The body is fixed to the cross by four nails, one through each foot and one through each hand. The head is slightly inclined, and the legs are not crossed, but hang down vertically.

This, then, is a typical example of the treatment of the Crucifixion in Byzantine art at the end of the sixth century. Although the accessories and minor details vary slightly, there was but little change in the main features of the scene until the eleventh century, after which time a marked alteration took place. The Saviour is represented after death has taken place instead of before[2]; the body is bent, the legs crossed, and a single spike substituted for the two nails through the feet; the eyes are closed, and the body is naked, with the exception of a cloth round the waist.

A very beautiful miniature illustrating the transition will be found in the Arundel Psalter in the British Museum, a MS. of the eleventh century.[3]

---

[1] Westwood's *Palæographia Pictoria Sacra*. The miniatures are engraved in Assemanus's work on the Florence Library, published in 1842. The Crucifixion forms the frontispiece of St. J. Tyrwhitt's *Art Teaching of the Primitive Church*.

[2] Martigny says (*Dict.*, p. 231) that the earliest example known of the Saviour shown dead on the cross is in a MS. written A.D. 1059, in the Laurentian Library at Florence.

[3] Brit. Mus., Arund. MS. No. 60, illustrated in Westwood's *Miniatures*, pl. 49.

The representations of the Crucifixion upon the Irish crosses were probably copied from the illuminations of the Celtic MSS., which in their turn were derived from the Byzantine or Greek MSS. There are at least three Irish MSS. containing illuminations of the Crucifixion, namely, the Psalter at St. John's College, Cambridge,[1] the Gospels (No. 51) at the Monastery of St. Gall in Switzerland,[2] and a MS. at Würtzburg in Bavaria.[3]

The drawing in the Psalter of St. John's College, Cambridge, is conventionalised in a most extraordinary manner, but, notwithstanding the extreme and almost barbarous rudeness of the figures, the essential elements of the Byzantine original are still preserved. Here, as in all the other early Crucifixions, only the arms and feet of the Saviour are destitute of clothing, but the drapery, instead of falling in graceful folds, consists of broad purple bands, with narrow yellow edges, swathed round the body, and interlaced so as to form knots. No attempt is made to follow the natural colouring of the objects represented,—the flesh-tints, for example, being a bright red, and the hair yellow. Anyone who has examined an Irish illuminated MS. critically must have been struck by the marked contrast between the high artistic merit of the ornamental features of the designs and the utter want of a sense of beauty exhibited in the figure-subjects. This anomaly can hardly be explained by supposing that the Irish illuminators had no good examples of figure-drawing to copy from, because the particular ways of treating different scenes corresponds with those adopted in Byzantine art, and the source which supplied the inspiration of the general arrangement of the pictures might also have been the means of suggesting improved methods of drawing. We can only conclude, therefore, either that the figures were purposely conventionalised from religious motives, so as not to appeal to the senses, and thus encourage idolatry ; or, what is more probable, that the object which the Celtic scribe had in view was not so much to produce a likeness of actual things as to exercise his wonderful powers of penmanship and give full scope to his exuberant fancy. Looked upon as a picture the result is a failure; but as a mosaic of brilliant colours and a pleasing combination of intricate

---

[1] Westwood's *Palæographia.*   [2] Westwood's *Miniatures.* pl. 28.
[3] *Archæologia*, vol. xliii, p. 141.

FIG. 32. - BRONZE PLATE WITH CRUCIFIXION.

From Athlone. Now in the museum of the Royal Irish Academy at Dublin

geometrical ornament, the miniature in an Irish MS. stands unrivalled. The human features, especially the ears, are ingeniously converted into spiral curves, beautiful as mere ornaments, but

Fig. 33.—Slab of Slate with Crucifixion, from old chapel on Calf of Man.

quite unlike the part of the body represented. The drapery is treated as a surface for the display of interlaced work, key-patterns, and the various kinds of Celtic decoration. Examples of this occur on three bronze plates in the Museum of the

Royal Irish Academy in Dublin,[1] and on a small slab of slate with a Crucifixion, found in the old chapel on the Calf of Man, and now in the possession of Mr. Quayle of Castletown, in the Isle of Man.[2] The latter is one of the most delicately executed pieces of sculpture I remember having seen, and almost resembles engraving. There is a circular wreath of interlaced work on the breast, and the whole of the drapery is covered with ornament. The stone is unfortunately broken, the figure of the sponge-bearer being wanting. Although found in the Isle of Man, the character of the art is distinctly Irish.

Irish Type of Crucifixion.

The leading features of the treatment of the Crucifixion in Ireland are as follows. The body of the Saviour is entirely draped, with the exception of the arms and feet, and is fastened to the cross with four nails, one through each hand and one through each of the feet. The eyes are shown open, and the limbs are extended perfectly straight along the three arms of the cross, whilst the head rests unbent against the fourth. In the MSS. there is sometimes a nimbus round the head of Christ, but it is not seen on the Irish crosses. At each side of the head of the Saviour, resting on the horizontal arms of the cross, is an angel, or sometimes a bird.[3] Angels occur on Byzantine ivories as accessories to the Crucifixion, but there is nothing in the Gospel narrative to warrant their introduction, unless, by a confusion of time and place, it is in reference to the angel that appeared to our Lord from heaven, strengthening Him (Luke xxii, 43) in the Agony in the Garden of Gethsemane.[4] Above the head of Christ, and sometimes beneath His feet, is a winged figure like a bird with a human head, intended either for the Holy Spirit, or the Angel of Victory, or perhaps the Phoenix.

The inscription over the head of the Saviour does not occur

---

[1] Stuart's *Sculptured Stones*, vol. ii, pl. 10 ; Westwood's *Miniatures*, pl. 51.

[2] Cumming's *Runic Remains of the Isle of Man*, fig. 30.

[3] In the Würtzburg MS. (*Archæologia*, vol. xliii, p. 141).

[4] Possibly the angels are introduced to show that the Crucifixion was witnessed by the hosts of heaven, in the same way that personifications of the Earth and Sea appear as witnesses of the scene.

on the Irish crosses, but it is found in the Würtzburg MS.
before referred to, being partly in Greek letters, thus: IHΣ XΠΣ.[1]
In this remarkable miniature are also the two thieves, with
good and evil spirits in the shape of birds ministering to each ;
below is a boat containing the Virgin, nimbed, and nine
other figures, underneath which is the cross with a pair of fish
at each side. This may either be one of the personifications of
the elements that witnessed the Crucifixion, as found on some

Fig. 34.—Crucifixion on Cross of SS. Patrick and Columba at Kells

ivories, or intended to symbolise the ship of the Church surrounded by the tempestuous waters of the world.

As a rule, the only actors in the scene of the Crucifixion, as
treated in Irish art, are the two soldiers, one piercing our
Lord's side with a spear, and the other offering Him a sponge,

[1] The Crucifixion in the Hiberno-Saxon Gospels in the Cathedral
Library at Durham is inscribed "HIC EST IHS REX IVDORVM". The
Crucifixion in the Saxon Psalter in the University Library at Cambridge
has the words LIGNVM VITAE inscribed on the arms of the cross.

L

or cup, shaped like a crescent, filled with vinegar, at the end of a reed. It is not stated in the Gospel of St. John (ch. xix, 34), who alone of the Four Evangelists describes the incident, which side was pierced, but on the Irish crosses it is generally shown as the left. There is an historical inaccuracy in representing our Lord's side being pierced before death had taken place, but the incident is introduced both as an instance of the fulfilment of prophecy and on account of its symbolical significance, having reference to the Sacraments of Baptism and the Lord's Supper. The apocryphal Gospel of Nicodemus,[1] which was used by the Church as early as the third century, tells us

Fig. 35.—Crucifixion on Metal Plates in the Museum of the Royal Irish Academy.

that the name of the soldier who pierced our Lord's side was Longinus, and we find it thus inscribed in the Hiberno-Saxon Gospels (No. A. ii, 17) in the Library of Durham Cathedral.[2] The name is evidently derived from the Greek λόγχη, a spear.

There is a curious legend concerning Longinus, that he struck Christ by accident, being blind, and that the blood of the Saviour fell upon his hand, which he lifted to his eye, and thus received his sight.[3] In the St. Gall Gospels (No. 51) the blood spurting into the eye of Longinus is indicated by a wavy line of red ink.[4] Another tradition asserts that Longinus and the centurion who exclaimed, " Truly this man was the Son of God "

[1] Hone's *Apocryphal New Testament*, ch. vii, 8.
[2] Westwood's *Miniatures*, p. 49.
[3] Mrs. Jameson's *Life of Our Lord*, vol. ii, p. 161.
[4] Westwood, pl. 48.

(Mark xv, 39), are one and the same person. The following passage will be found in Ælfric's " Uplifting of the Holy Rood" (Brit. Mus. MS., Jul. E. vii), translated by R. Morris in the

Fig. 36.—Crucifixion, from the St. Gall Gospels.

Legends of the Holy Rood, published by the Early English Text Society, p. 106:—" The Saviour is so merciful that He would have mercy upon His own murderers if they would turn and pray for His mercy, as many of them did; for instance, the centurion who wickedly pierced Him (Christ) in His holy side and afterwards turned to Him. The centurion was named Longinus." This may account for the absence of so important a witness of the Crucifixion as the centurion from most of the early representations. That the same man should strike Christ and yet believe that He was the Son of God, is improbable, unless we accept the explanation that he used his spear inadvertently, as related in the legend. The name of the sponge-bearer is said by tradition to be Stephaton, and is so inscribed on a wall-painting of the tenth century in the Chapel of Saint-Remy-la-Varenne (Maine et Loire),[1] and on an ivory plaque of the tenth century in the Kunst Kammer at Berlin, a cast of which is in the South Kensington Museum (Westwood's *Catal.*, No. 132).

The Alpha and Omega symbol is used in connection with the Crucifixion. It occurs in the Hiberno-Saxon Gospels at Durham; the Greek letters, of large size, being inscribed in red ink on each side of the head of the Saviour, whilst above the two four-winged angels are written the words "Initium et Finis". The Alpha and Omega is also to be seen on the two ends of the horizontal arms of the cross on an ivory plaque of Irish or Anglo-Saxon origin in the South Kensington Museum,[2] representing the descent from the cross. In this instance there is a skull at the foot of the cross, in reference to the name Golgotha, and the tradition that the cross grew out of Adam's grave.[3]

Upon some of the Irish crosses, as at Moone Abbey, co. Kildare, the Crucifixion is represented without any accessories or other figures besides that of the Saviour. This is universally the case upon the early churchyard crosses of Cornwall, which are made out of hard granite, and sculptured in the rudest possible manner. The crucified Saviour, without accessories, also occurs on the key-stones of the doorways of the round towers at Donoughmore, co. Meath, and Brechin in Forfarshire. There is a fine example of the same method of treatment on a cross ornamented with interlaced work at Kirkburton, in Yorkshire.

---

[1] Didron's *Manuel d'Iconographie Chrétienne Greque et Latine*, p. 196.
[2] No. 3-72.
[3] J. P. Berjeau. *History of the Holy Cross.*

Scotch Type of Crucifixion.

Upon the sculptured stones of Scotland the Crucifixion is a very rare subject, there being only two instances known, one in the Edinburgh Museum of Antiquities from Monifieth in For-

Fig. 37.—Crucifixion on Sculptured Stones at (1) Kirkholm and (2) at Monifieth.

farshire,[1] and the other at Kirkholm in Wigtonshire.[2] The top of the Monifieth stone is broken off, so that only the lower portion of the body of the Saviour remains. The drapery extends

[1] Stuart's *Sculptured Stones of Scotland*, vol. ii, pl. 80.
[2] *Ibid.*, vol. ii, pl. 70. Dr. Joseph Anderson informs me that there is a representation of the Crucifixion upon the Cross at Camuston, in Forfarshire, illustrated in Stuart's *Sculptured Stones of Scotland*, vol. i, pl. 87 ; but the engraving there given is so bad that it is impossible to make out the subject.

almost down to the knees, and the legs are not crossed, but fixed with two nails. On the right is a figure holding a book, and on the left a figure with the hands crossed over the breast. These may perhaps be intended for the Virgin Mary and St. John. Below are three panels, the upper one containing a pair of figures with staves; the next, two men with horns in their right hands; and the bottom one, a man seated, playing a harp.

King David playing the Harp.—There is some reason to suppose that the latter may represent the Psalmist; for, setting aside the view that secular scenes are portrayed upon Christian monuments as being untenable, because not in accordance with experience, there are only a certain limited number of passages in the Bible to choose from which refer to the use of the harp. The most important texts are the one which describes the son of Jesse as being chosen to play before Saul, because he was a cunning player on an harp (Samuel xvi, 16); the ones mentioning David's four assistants, Asaph, Heman, Jeduthun (1 Chron. xxv, 1), and Ethan (1 Chron. vi, 44); the numerous verses in the Psalms; and the one in the Revelations (ch. v, 8), telling how the four beasts and the four and twenty elders fell down before the Lamb, every one of them having " harps and golden vials full of odours, which are the prayers of saints." The scene from the Revelations belongs to the subject of Christ in Glory, which is sculptured on the back of the cross of Muiredach at Clonmacnois, and will be described further on. King David playing on the harp is generally the miniature which forms the frontispiece of the early Irish and Saxon Psalters, as for instance in an Irish MS. of the ninth century in the British Museum (Vit. F. xi),[1] where David is alone; and in the Saxon MS. of the eleventh century, in the Cambridge University Library (F. f. 1, 23),[2] where he is accompanied by his four assistants, with the names DAVID REX—ASAPH—EMAN—ETHAN —IDITHVN, inscribed over each. In the latter, the Spirit of God inspiring the Psalmist (1 Samuel vi, 13) is shown as a bird. The same thing occurs in a Saxon MS. of the eleventh century in the British Museum (Tib. C. vi),[3] on the back of the

---

[1] Westwood's *Miniatures*, pl. 51, fig. 6; and for other examples, see pls. 3, 18, and 37.   [2] Westwood's *Palæographia*, No. 41.

[3] Miss Twining's *Christian Symbols and Emblems*, pl. 31.

cross of Muiredach at Clonmacnois, and on the end of the Irish
shrine of St. Moedog, in the Museum of the Royal Irish Academy
at Dublin.[1]

Whether the figure playing the harp on the Monifieth stone
is intended for David or not, there should be no reason for
doubting that such is the case on the grounds of the appropri-
ateness of the subject. David is, perhaps, the most important
of all the Old Testament types of Christ, for reasons which
must be familiar to everyone,—such as the frequent references
in the Gospels to our Lord's descent from David, and because
of the prophecies relating to the Crucifixion in the Psalms.
The *Biblia Pauperum* and *Speculum Humanæ Salvationis* of
later mediæval times are full of instances of the close analogies
which were supposed to exist between the events in the lives of
David and Christ.

The harper on the Monifieth stone is not an isolated example,
for there is an exactly similar figure upon the cross at Dupplin
Castle, in Perthshire.[2] A harp without anyone playing on it is
to be seen on the cross-slabs at Nigg[3] in Ross-shire, and at
Aldbar in Forfarshire,[4] in both cases associated with a sheep or
ram, probably indicating David's being called away from his
pastoral calling to play before Saul (1 Samuel xvi, 19). There
are other representations of harpers on Irish crosses at Ullard,
co. Carlow[5]; Castle Dermot, co. Kildare, and on the cross of
Fland at Clonmacnois, King's County.[6] In the last instance
the figure is more like that of a female than a male, and seems
to be riding on the back of an animal. On the cross of Maelmor,
at Kirkmichael[7] in the Isle of Man, there is a harper, and at
the side a figure holding a horn. What makes it more probable
that the harper is intended for David, is that other scenes from
the life of David—such as his contest with the lion—are also

[1] *Archæologia*, vol. xliii, p. 131. A man playing a harp also occurs on
the cover of the Stowe Missal (see O'Conor, *Rerum Hibern. Script.*).

[2] Stuart's *Sculptured Stones of Scotland*, vol. i, pl. 58.

[3] *Ibid.*, vol. i, pl. 29. Examples also occur on late West Highland slabs
at Keils and Iona. See vol. ii, pls. 57 and 62.

[4] *Ibid.*, vol. i, pl. 82.

[5] O'Neill's *Irish Crosses*, pl. 9.

[6] *Ibid.*, pl. 24.

[7] Cumming's *Crosses of the Isle of Man*, fig. 28a.

found on the sculptured stones. In the MSS. David is generally shown crowned, but this is not the case in the Irish Psalter in the British Museum (Vit. F. xi), so that it is not without precedent that he should be represented uncrowned on the stones.

Figures holding horns.—Immediately over the harper upon the Monifieth stone are two figures with horns in their hands.

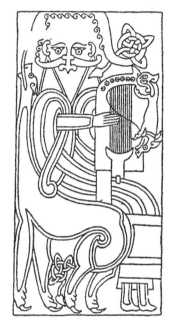

Fig. 38.—David and Goliath, and David playing on the Harp, from the Irish Psalter in the British Museum. (Vit. F. xi.)

This is the only representation of the kind in Scotland, but on the cross of Maelmor, at Kirkmichael in the Isle of Man, is a man holding a horn in front of a harper; at Llangan, in Glamorganshire, there is a man with a horn below the Crucifixion; and other instances occur at Eyam and Bakewell in Derbyshire. In the contemporary MSS. the only scene in which a horn appears is in the Anointing of David by Samuel (Samuel xvi, 13), as in the Greek Psalter written in the year A.D. 1066 (Brit. Mus., Add. MS. 19,352); in the Saxon Psalter of the eleventh cent. (Brit. Mus., Tib. C. vi), and in the English Psalter (Brit. Mus., Nero C. iv). In the Saxon MS. (Tib. C. vi) the Hand of God is shown holding a horn above the head of King David playing on the harp. Throughout the whole of the Bible there are continual references to the word horn used in a figurative sense, as when Hannah says, "Mine horn is exalted in the Lord" (1 Samuel ii, 1) ; and when Zacharias blesses the

Fig. 39.—Crucifixion on Cross at Llangan.

Lord, who " hath raised up an horn of Salvation for us, in the house of his servant David".

The above passages from Scripture are merely quoted to show what portions bear upon the subject under consideration, but it must be clearly understood that the apparent fitness of certain texts to explain symbolic scenes and objects represented in Christian art, does not in any way amount to proof that the analogies which seem clear to us were perceived by the early

Celtic sculptors. In order to complete the chain of evidence, it is necessary either to show by reference to the literature of the time what parts of the Bible were then singled out specially for comment, and how the words were interpreted; or to prove, by the study of the pictures in contemporary MSS. and such representations as are inscribed, that particular subjects were treated in a certain conventional way, and no other. According to the amount of evidence forthcoming, we shall therefore have scenes of which there is a satisfactory explanation; those which cannot be interpreted at all; and, between the two, meanings suggested as being either possible or probable. The weight of the evidence should always be considered, and there should never be any confusion between what is only a working hypothesis and proved facts.

After this somewhat lengthy digression, we will now return to the subject of the Crucifixion.

Besides the stone at Monifieth there is one other in Scotland which has the Crucifixion upon it, at Kirkholm in Wigtonshire.[1] The monument in question is a slab of grey whinstone, with crosses of the same shape on both back and front, one side being ornamented with scrolls of foliage and interlaced work, and the other having a very rude design incised upon it, consisting of the Saviour on the cross, with the figure of a man below in the centre, having two birds on his right, and a pair of pincers and a rectangular object on his left. It has been suggested by Dr. Stuart[2] that the pair of pincers is one of the emblems of the Passion; but it must be observed that although the pincers for extracting the nails from the Saviour's feet appears in the scene of the Descent from the Cross as early as the twelfth century,[3] the use of this instrument as a symbol by itself belongs to a much later period of art. A pair of pincers occurs on the cross at Dunfallandy in Perthshire,[4] and also at Halton in Lancashire.

---

[1] Stuart's *Sculptured Stones*, vol. ii, pl. 70. It came originally from the Chapel of Kilmorie, and was afterwards built into the walls of the parish church, whence it was removed to the house of Corsewell.

[2] *Sculptured Stones*, vol. ii, p. 34.

[3] On capital of column of chancel-arch, south side, at Adel Church, Yorkshire.   [4] Stuart's *Sculptured Stones*, vol. i, pl. 47.

Saxon Type of Crucifixion.

The treatment of the Crucifixion upon the Saxon sculptured stones in England differs in some particulars from the conventional representations found in Ireland, Scotland, and Wales, which we have already described as being of one type, having as leading features the fully draped figure of the Saviour, with

Fig. 40.—Crucifixion on Cross at Sandbach.

unbent body and limbs, the four nails, the angels above, and the sponge and spear-bearers below. The chief modifications introduced into the Saxon Crucifixions are, that instead of the body being draped in a tunic without sleeves, there is only a cloth girt round the waist; that the sun and moon occupy the places of the angels above the cross; and that in some cases the feet of the Saviour are supported on a suppedaneum, and the

Virgin Mary and St. John stand at the foot of the cross, the soldiers with the spear and sponge being omitted. The head of the Saviour is almost always nimbed. Examples of the Crucifixion, with the sun and moon above and the soldiers with the sponge and spear-bearers below, exist on crosses with Hiberno-Saxon forms of ornaments at Aycliffe in Durham, Alnmouth in Northumberland, and Bradbourne in Derbyshire. On the cross at Sandbach in Cheshire the Crucifixion is surrounded by the symbols of the four Evangelists, and Sol and Luna, placed side by side on the top arm of the cross above the head of our Lord.

It is generally believed that the sun and moon are introduced in the scene of the Crucifixion to signify that there was darkness over the whole earth from the sixth to the ninth hour, as told by St. Matthew (ch. xxvii, 45), St. Mark (ch. xv, 33), and St. Luke (ch. xxiii, 44). St. Luke mentions specially that the sun was darkened; and we learn from the apocryphal Gospel of Nicodemus (viii, 10) that the Jews explained to the governor that an eclipse of the sun had happened according to its usual custom.

Martigny[1] believes the sun and moon to be symbolical of the Godhead and Manhood of Christ, and supports his view by quotations from the Fathers, and by pointing out that the sun and moon are shown in other scenes besides, such as the Resurrection of Lazarus, on each side of the Good Shepherd, and on the corners of sarcophagi. The sun alone occurs in representations of the Harrowing of Hell,[2] probably in reference to the words, "O Lord, thou hast set the ensigns of thy glory in heaven", in the chapter describing it in the apocryphal Gospel of Nicodemus (xix, 10).

The sun and moon are represented in several different ways, but, as in the case of the personifications of rivers and signs of the zodiac, classical models have been so closely adhered to that, except for the distinctly Christian character of the rest, they might be the work of a pagan artist. The sun is shown as a male figure, crowned, and with beams of light radiating from

[1] *Dict. des Ant. Chrét.*, pp. 230 and 739.
[2] On tympanum of Norman doorway at Quenington, Gloucestershire. Brit. Mus. MS., Tib. C. vi, and Nero C. iv.

his head, and holding a flaming torch. The moon is a female figure, also holding a lighted torch, and with a crescent on her forehead. Sometimes the sun is in his chariot drawn by horses, and the moon in hers drawn by bulls.[1]

On the sculptured stones the busts of the sun and moon are enclosed within circular medallions, and the carving has, in most cases, altogether disappeared. The position of Sol and Luna varies, being most commonly placed in the blank spaces above the side arms of the cross, but sometimes on the top arm of the cross, either side by side or one above the other. There are two very beautiful examples of the Crucifixion, with the sun and moon, in the Saxon Psalter in the British Museum (Tib. D. xxvii),[2] and the Great Psalter in the Boulogne Public Library,[3] both written about the end of the tenth or beginning of the eleventh century. In the Boulogne Psalter[4] there is the superscription IIIC XPC over the head of the Saviour, and the feet are supported on a block. Below, on the left, piercing the Saviour's right side, is the soldier with the spear, and on the other the sponge-bearer, carrying in one hand the vessel full of vinegar, mentioned by St. John (xix, 29) only out of the Four Evangelists, who says that the vinegar was sprinkled with a plant called hyssop dipped in it, whereas St. Matthew and St. Mark mention a sponge on a reed, and St. Luke omits the incident altogether. On the right of the picture is St. John holding a book, and on the left the Virgin Mary with her hands extended. Built into the walls of the Saxon Church of Daglingworth in Gloucestershire, above the chancel-arch, is a slab on which is sculptured a Crucifixion, perhaps of the eleventh century, showing a vessel of vinegar and the hyssop, and a scourge in the hand of the soldier with the spear.

The miniature of the Crucifixion in the Saxon Psalter in the

[1] See beautiful miniature in Saxon Astronomical Treatise of Aratus (eleventh century), Brit. Mus., Tib. B. v, in Westwood's *Miniatures*, pl. 48.

[2] Written (A.D. 978-998) by Ælsine, a monk of New Minster, for Ælfwine, afterwards abbot of that monastery (A.D. 1035).

[3] Written (*circa* A.D. 1003) by Heriveus, and illuminated by Odbert, in the Monastery of St. Bertin.

[4] Westwood's *Miniatures*, pl. 39.

British Museum (Titus D. xxvii)[1] is similar to that in the Boulogne Psalter, except that the soldiers with the spear and sponge are wanting, and at the top of the cross is a hand issuing from a cloud, in the attitude of giving the benediction. The names are inscribed as follows: SOL . LUNA . $\overline{\text{SCA}}$ MARIA . $\overline{\text{SCS}}$ IOHANNES ; and the title, HIC EST IHC NAZARENUS REX IUDEOR.

Fig. 41.—Crucifixion on slab built into walls of Saxon Church at Daglingworth.

Upon the magnificent cross at Gosforth in Cumberland,[2] a good cast of which may be seen in the South Kensington Museum, there is a Crucifixion presenting some exceptional features. The figure of the Saviour with arms extended is enclosed within a rectangular frame of cable moulding. Outside this frame below are two figures: on the left, the soldier piercing our Lord's right side, and causing a triple stream of blood to

[1] W. de G. Birch's *Early Drawings and Illuminations in the British Museum.*

[2] Stuart's *Sculptured Stones,* vol. ii, pl. 24 ; and *Journ. Brit. Archæol. Inst.,* vol. xl, p. 143.

issue,[1] with a spear which passes over the side of the frame; and on the right, a female in a dress reaching to the feet, and with a long plait of hair behind and holding an object in her hand. I can recall very few instances in early art where the spear-bearer is unaccompanied by the sponge-bearer.[2] The female figure is probably one of the women mentioned in the Gospel account, and the object in her hand may be a vessel containing the spices and ointments for the burial.[3]

The finest conception of the Crucifixion in Saxon art, and the earliest instance of the Saviour being represented after He had bowed His head and given up the ghost, is to be found in a Psalter in the British Museum (Harl. 2,904),[4] which Professor Westwood attributes to the end of the tenth century, from its similarity to the Winchester Books of St. Æthelwold. The head of the Saviour, which is surrounded by a cruciferous nimbus, is inclined to the left, and the eyes are closed. The body is slightly bent, the arms hanging down a little below the horizontal arms of the cross, but the legs perfectly straight. Instead of the nails, the five wounds, with triple streams of blood, are shown, one in each hand, one in each foot, and the other in the right side. The feet are supported on a square block. The drapery consists of a cloth girt round the waist; over the head is the title, " HIC EST NAZAREN IHC REX IUDEOR."

Below, on the right of the picture, is St. John holding a pen, and a scroll inscribed, " Hic· est Discipulus qui testimoniū perhibet", in reference to the words of the Evangelist (John xix, 35),—" And he that saw it bare record, and his record is true : and he knoweth that he saith true, that ȳe might believe."

---

[1] The triple stream, indicated by three wavy red lines, is to be seen in the Saxon MS. in the British Museum (Harl. MS. 2904).

[2] On the Norman font at Lenton, Notts, the soldier with the spear occurs alone.

[3] The Three Maries, carrying boxes of spices for embalming the body, usually occur in the scene of the visit to the Sepulchre, not at the Crucifixion. In the Boulogne Psalter, previously referred to, the Three Maries at the Sepulchre are shown immediately below the Crucifixion, and one of the women carries a vessel shaped like a horn, and the other two round boxes.

[4] Westwood's *Miniatures*, pl. 43.

On the left is the Virgin Mary, with a hood over her head and holding a cloak in front of her face. Both figures have the nimbus round the head. The drapery is drawn in the peculiar fluttering style of late Anglo-Saxon art, and the Virgin has that curious hump-backed appearance which is so common in drawings of the period.

The latest Anglo-Saxon Crucifixion, and the one which comes nearest to the true mediæval type, is to be found in the Arundel Psalter (No. 60)[1] in the British Museum, a MS. of the eleventh century. It differs from the preceding one in having the knees bent and the whole body inclined. The wounds in the hands and right side are shown, but the feet have the two spikes through them. On each side below is a conventional tree, and at the four corners are the symbols of the Four Evangelists. The only further modification introduced subsequently was the substitution of one nail through the feet in place of two, with the crossing of the legs.

Upon some of the Irish crosses the crucified Saviour wears a crown, as at Graigue-na-managh, co. Kilkenny,[2] Tuam, co. Galway,[3] and Glendalough, co. Wicklow. The only crown mentioned in the Gospels is that of thorns, but in the Revelations (xiv, 14) the Son of Man is described as wearing a golden crown; and in other parts of the New Testament the word is used in a figurative sense—a crown of life, of glory, of righteousness, and an incorruptible crown. The idea is fully brought out in a painting of the Crucifixion in the Chapel of St. Silvestro at Rome,[4] where an angel is seen changing the crown of thorns for a real one. Figures of the crucified Saviour wearing a crown belong generally to the twelfth century, and are seen in Limoges enamels.[5]

The Dextera Dei.

In describing the miniature of the Crucifixion in the Saxon Psalter in the British Museum (Titus D. xxvii), we have

---

[1] Westwood's *Miniatures*, pl. 49.

[2] O'Neill's *Irish Crosses*, pl. 9.

[3] *Ibid.*, pl. 12.

[4] Mrs. Jameson's *History of Our Lord*, vol. ii, p. 175.

[5] *Ibid.*, vol. ii, p. 334, crucifix belonging to Lord Zouche. Also Marcus Keane's *Towers and Temples of Ireland*, p. 167.

already referred to a hand issuing from a cloud at the top of
the cross. This symbol is used throughout the whole range of
early Christian art to express the First Person of the Trinity.
It has its origin in the innumerable texts of the Old Testament,
especially in the Psalms, which speak of the Hand of God, and
such passages in the New as the one where St. Peter, on the
Day of Pentecost, says that Jesus was "by the right hand of
God exalted" (Acts ii, 23).

Thus, in any scene where the power of God is specially
manifested, or where the Almighty is described in the Bible as
holding direct intercourse with man, the Hand symbol is used.
Such scenes are far more common in the Old Testament than
in the New; for in the earlier stages of the world's history God
saw fit to control human affairs by communicating openly
with His chosen agents, but afterwards He made His unseen
influence felt by inspired prophets, and through His Son, inter-
vening only at rare intervals. Although there are so many
passages in the Old Testament describing God's dealing with
man, only a limited number are selected for illustration in
Christian art, either as typifying or setting forth in some striking
way the doctrines of the new dispensation.

The principal scenes in which the Hand symbol occurs are
as follows :—

In the Old Testament.

Offerings of Cain and Abel (Gen. iv, 9).
Sacrifice of Isaac (Gen. xxii, 11).
Moses and the Burning Bush (Exod. iii, 4).
Moses receiving the Law (Exod. xix, 19).

In the New Testament.

Flight into Egypt (Matt. ii, 13).
Baptism of Christ (Matt. iii, 17).
Transfiguration (Matt. xvii, 5).
Agony in Gethsemane (Matt. xxvi, 39).
Crucifixion (Matt. xxvii, 36).
Ascension (Acts i, 11).
Christ in Glory (Rev. iv, 1).
Story of Ananias and Sapphira (Acts v, 4)
Martyrdom of Stephen (Acts vii, 59).
St. Michael and the Dragon (Rev. xii, 10).

In all these cases there is a distinct text of Scripture, which is given above, describing God as holding direct communication with man, or man appealing to God.

In the scenes of the Sacrifice of Isaac,[1] Moses and the Burning Bush, and Moses receiving the Law, all of which are found amongst the paintings in the Catacombs, the Hand symbol is made to stand for the First Person of the Trinity; but in the scene of the Offerings of Cain and Abel, the earliest examples of which occur on the sculptured sarcophagi, God is represented as an aged man. In later times, however, the Hand symbol[2]

Fig. 42.—Christ in Glory, with Hand Symbol, on Tympanum at Elkstone.

is used instead of God in His human form addressing Cain and Abel.

An instance of the Hand symbol in the scene of the Flight into Egypt exists on one of the sculptured capitals of the twelfth century, at St. Benoît sur Loire, in France.[3] Although the presence of all three Persons of the Trinity at the Baptism of Christ is distinctly specified in the Gospels, it is seldom that

[1] As on tympanum of Norman doorway at Rochester Cathedral.

[2] As in Cædmon's *Saxon Paraphrase of the Scriptures*, in the Bodleian Library at Oxford (*Archæologia*, vol. xxiv, pl. 76); and on the eleventh century bronze doors of Augsburg Cathedral (cast in South Kensington Museum).

[3] De Caumont, *Abécédaire d'Archéologie*, p. 257.

more than two are represented in art, and the Holy Spirit as the dove is far more common than the Hand symbol placed above the head of the Saviour.[1] Examples of the Hand symbol at the Transfiguration,[2] the Agony in Gethsemane,[3] and the Ascension,[4] are to be seen on early ivories; Christ in Glory on the tympanum of the Norman doorway at Elkstone, Gloucestershire; St. Michael and the Dragon on the Norman tympanum at Hoveringham, Notts; the Story of Ananias and Sapphira[5] on the Brescia Casket; the Martrydom of Stephen on a bronze plate engraved by Gori.[6]

Fig. 43.—St. Michael and the Dragon, with Hand Symbol, on Tympanum at Hoveringham.

The Hand symbol at the Crucifixion refers to our Lord's words (Luke xxiii, 46), "Father, into thy hands I commend my spirit." It is to be seen upon two of the high crosses of Ireland, namely, that of Muiredach at Monasterboice,[7] and that of

[1] The dove and the Dextera Dei occur together above the head of Christ on a few Carlovingian ivories. (Westwood's *Catal. of Fictile Ivories in S. K. Mus.*, Nos. 240, 275, 277.)

[2] S. K. Mus. Ivory, No. 256, 1867. (See Maskell's *Catal.*)

[3] S. K. Mus. Cast. (Westwood's *Catal.*, No. 349.)

[4] S. K. Mus. Ivory, No. 258, 1867.

[5] This is, I believe, a unique subject. (See Westwood, *Catal.*, No. 94; and Garrucci, *Storia del Arte Cristiana*, vol. vi, pl. 441.)

[6] See Martigny's *Dict.*, art. "Étienne".

[7] O'Neill's *Irish Crosses*, pl. 15.

King Fland at Clonmacnois.[1] In both cases the hand is surrounded by an ornamental nimbus; but instead of being over the Crucifixion, as is usually the case, the Hand symbol is carved on the under-side of the projecting arm of the cross, at Monasterboice to the left of the Crucifixion, and at Clonmacnois to the right. The effect produced is remarkable, for when the spectator stands beneath the cross and looks up he sees the Hand of God immediately above his head, as if issuing from heaven. The corresponding arms of the crosses on the other

Fig. 44.—Hand Symbol on Cross of Muiredach at Monasterboice.

side are in both cases ornamented with animal forms. A fine example of the Hand symbol above the Crucifixion in Norman sculpture exists at Romsey Abbey, in Hampshire.[2] Upon one of the panels of the cross in the town of Kells, co. Meath,[3] the Hand symbol occurs in front of a tall, bearded man holding a large rectangular object in each hand, and with two small kneeling figures below. I am unable to interpret the meaning of this scene.

The Hand symbol, with the inscription DEXTERA DĪ, forms one of the principal ornaments upon the maniple found in the tomb

[1] O'Neill's *Irish Crosses*, pl. 24. At Bishop Auckland, Yorkshire, is a Saxon stone with the cross within a circle and the Hand symbol above it.
[2] Twining's *Christian Symbols and Emblems*, pl. 2.
[3] O'Neill's *Irish Crosses*, pl. 34.

of St. Cuthbert at Durham, which was made by Queen Ælflæd for Frithestan, Bishop of Winchester (A.D. 904-916).[1] It is also to be seen on the Bayeux Tapestry,[2] above the church of St. Peter. The object in this case seems to have been to show that the blessing of God was specially bestowed upon the consecrated building, for the same symbol, with the inscription DEX(TERA), is also placed over a sculpture at Le Mans in France,[3] on the

Fig. 45.—Hand Symbol over Crucifix, at Romsey Abbey.

church of that town, with the patron saints, SS. Gervais and Protais, on either side. We see the same thing again in the consecration of St. Martin of Tours, on a tapestry of the thirteenth century in the Louvre.[4] The Hand symbol is found on almost every page of the Utrecht Psalter, in which the words of the

[1] J. Raine's *St. Cuthbert.* Other Saxon examples are to be met with upon the coins of Eadward the Elder, and Æthelred II.

[2] *Vetusta Monumenta,* vol. vi, pl. 7; and *Bayeux Tapestry,* published for the Arundel Society by F. R. Fowke.

[3] Martigny's *Dict.,* p. 247.

[4] Lacroix, *Military and Religious Life of the Middle Ages,* p. 281.

Psalmist are rendered literally,[1] and it is to be seen very frequently in Ælfric's Saxon Heptateuch[2] in the British Museum (Claud. B. iv).

There are a great many varieties of this symbol, as regards the position of the hand, the attitude of the fingers, and the action performed. The position of the hand is generally facing either upwards or downwards in the centre of the picture, or inclined diagonally from one of the upper corners. The attitude of the fingers is either that of giving the benediction, or outstretched, with the fingers sometimes close together, and sometimes apart.[3] In many instances a cruciferous nimbus surrounds the hand,[4] or the Alpha and Omega are added,[5] or rays of power are seen issuing from the tips of the fingers.[6] The actions performed by the hand are,—holding back the knife in Abraham's hand; presenting the Tables of the Law to Moses; crowning saints with wreaths[7]; casting down great stones from heaven upon the Amorites (Joshua x, 11)[8]; holding the horn of oil for the anointing of David[9]; grasping a bundle of arrows, in illustration of the verse of the Psalms (xviii, 14), "Yea he sent out his arrows and scattered them; and he shot out lightnings, and discomfited them";[10] and holding the scales in which St. Michael weighs the souls[11]; extended to Christ when ascending into

[1] W. de Gray Birch's *Utrecht Psalter.*

[2] Illustrating text, "Then men began to call upon the name of the Lord" (Gen. ii, 19); Abraham worshipping at altars at Bethel and Mamre; Abraham rescuing Lot after the battle of four kings against five; Abraham's vision of the lamp, etc.

[3] Miss Twining's *Christian Symbols and Emblems*, pls. 1 and 2.

[4] Doorway of Ferrara Cathedral, twelfth century.

[5] Doorway of Church of St. Peter at Vienne. (De Caumont's *Abécédaire d'Archéologie*, p. 20.)

[6] Above head of Charles the Bald, in his Bible, in the Imp. Lib., Paris; in the scene of the Martyrdom of Stephen, already mentioned; and over the head of the Prophet Isaiah in the Greek Psalter of the tenth century, in the Paris Library, No. 130. (Didron's *Christian Iconography*, by Miss Stokes, vol. i, p. 202.)

[7] Chiefly on mosaics of seventh century at Rome.

[8] Mosaic in the Church of Galla Placidia, Ravenna.

[9] Saxon MS., Brit. Mus. (Tib. C. vi).

[10] *Ibid.* (Harl. 603).

[11] Tympanum of doorway of Autun Cathedral. (De Caumont *Abécédaire*, p. 248.)

heaven[1]; holding the scroll of the Gospel of St. Mark to the Evangelist.[2] In fact, whenever the Almighty speaks with man, guides, protects, defends, blesses, or is appealed to by His chosen people, or avenges Himself on the wicked, there the Hand symbol appears as the outward and visible form under which His power is manifested.

All attempts to symbolise the Creator of the Universe, except in the most abstract manner, are both unscriptural and profane; for nothing can be plainer than the views held on the subject by the inspired writers, both of the Old and New Testament. Jacob, indeed, was privileged above others, and says, " I have seen God face to face, and my life is preserved" (Genesis xxxii, 30). On Mount Sinai, " The Lord said unto Moses, Go down, charge the people, lest they break through unto the Lord to gaze, and many of them perish" (Exodus xix, 21). " Manoah said unto his wife, We shall surely die, because we have seen God." St. John tells us (i, 18), " No man hath seen God at any time"; and (iv, 24), " God is a Spirit." The early Christians, during the first four centuries, adhered to the Scriptural view of the case, and the First Person of the Trinity was almost always symbolised by the hand[3]; but, from about the ninth century onwards, the difficulty of representing God as man, without diminishing those feelings of awe-and reverence which would naturally deter the artist from approaching so sacred a subject, was avoided by assuming the identity between God the Father and God the Son. The Almighty is thus shown as a bearded man, with the cruciferous nimbus round the head ; and, except for the surroundings, there is no means of distinguishing between the figure of the Creator and that of Christ. In the Saxon Psalter of the eleventh century in the British Museum (Tib. C. vi),[4] in the miniature of the Trinity all three Persons have the cruciferous nimbus, God the Father in the centre in human form, holding a book, and giving the benediction, having

---

[1] Saxon Benedictional of Æthelwold, circa 975 (Westwood's Miniatures, pl. 45) ; and on Ivories, Mrs. Jameson's Life of Our Lord, vol. ii, pp. 263 and 307.

[2] Saxon MS., Brit. Mus. (Royal iE vi), Westwood's Miniatures, pl. 15.

[3] On some of the sculptured sarcophagi at Rome the First Person of the Trinity creating Eve is represented as an aged man.

[4] Miss Twining's Christian Symbols and Emblems, pl. 34.

the letters Alpha and Omega at each side of the head; on His right hand is God the Son as the Lamb, and on His left God the Holy Ghost as the Dove. In MSS. of this period the Almighty creating the world is also represented as Christ[1]; but where the identity between the Father and Son is shown in the most striking manner is in the illuminated initial letter D of the 110th Psalm, beginning, "The Lord said unto my Lord, Sit thou on my right hand until I make thine enemies thy footstool."[2]

In the miniature of St. Matthew in the Lindisfarne Gospels in the British Museum[3] (*circa* A.D. 710), the head of a man with a plain nimbus, and holding a book, protrudes from behind a curtain, to signify God inspiring the Evangelist, who is taking down the words in an open volume before him.

The last stage of the degradation of symbolism was reached in the sixteenth century, when we find the Almighty in the guise of a human being, arrayed in pontifical robes and tiara[4]; and the paintings of Raphael in the Vatican of the Creator as a man,[5] however great their merit as works of art, cannot fail to shock the finer sensibilities of the more spiritually minded.

Christ in Glory at the Transfiguration, the Ascension, the Second Advent, and the Last Judgment.

It has been already stated that the central subject on the back of the cross of Muiredach at Monasterboice, corresponding with the Crucifixion on the front, is the Last Judgment.[6] The chief features in the scene are the figure of Christ in the middle, with the righteous on His right hand and the wicked on His left, whilst below is St. Michael weighing the souls. The Saviour holds in His left hand the cross, symbolising His

---

[1] Saxon MS., eleventh century, Brit. Mus. (Tib. C. vi), Mrs. Jameson's *Life of Our Lord*, vol. i, p. 72 ; also on an ivory of the ninth century, in the Douce Collection (Westwood's *Catal.*, No. 147, and Didron's *Christian Iconography*, vol. i, p. 173).

[2] Thirteenth Century Psalters in Brit. Mus. (Ar. 83 and 157) ; Twining's *Christian Symbols and Emblems*, pl. 37.

[3] Westwood's *Miniatures*, pl. 13.

[4] Didron's *Christian Iconography*, by Miss M. Stokes, vol. i, p. 218.

[5] Mrs. Jameson's *Life of Our Lord*, vol. i, p. 85.

[6] O'Neill's *Irish Crosses*, pl. 10.

Passion, and in the right a floriated sceptre, to signify His triumph. This method of representing Christ in Glory seems to be peculiar to Celtic art in Ireland, and occurs upon six of the more important high crosses.[1]

The figure in the Irish MSS. which most nearly resembles that of Christ in Glory, as shown on the crosses, is the miniature

Fig. 46.—Christ in Glory on the Cross of SS. Patrick and Columba at Kells.

of St. Luke, in the Gospels of St. Chad, of the eighth century, in the Cathedral library at Lichfield.[2] If it were not for the symbol of the Bull above the head of St. Luke, it might be supposed that the picture was intended to represent Christ, for upon the nimbus are three crosses, formed of red dots, and in the right hand he holds a sceptre, terminating in spiral scrolls of interlaced branches, bearing green leaves like the shamrock,

[1] At Monasterboice, Termonfechin, Clonmacnois, Kells, Arboe, Drumcliff. (O'Neill's *Irish Crosses*, pls. 10, 16, 22, 28, 31.)

[2] Westwood's *Palæographia*, and Palæog. Soc. Publ., pl. 21.

and in the left a cross. Floriated sceptres are to be seen in the
hands of angels and men in the *Book of Kells*,[1] in the library of

Fig. 47.—Miniature of St. Luke, from St. Chad's Gospels.

Trinity College ; on the metal shrine of St. Moedoc,[2] in the

[1] Miniatures of Virgin and Child (Westwood's *Palæographia*) and St.
Luke (Westwood's *Miniatures*, pl. 10).
[2] Westwood's *Miniatures*, pl. 52, figs. 5 and 6.

museum of the Royal Irish Academy at Dublin; and on one of the crosses at St. Vigeans in Forfarshire. There is only one

Fig. 48.—Enthroned figures holding floriated Sceptres on Cross at St. Vigeans, Forfarshire.

instance known of the picture of Christ in Glory in an Irish MS., and that is in the Gospels (No. 51) in the library of St. Gall in Switzerland.[1]   The treatment of the scene differs from that

[1] Westwood's *Miniatures*, pl. 27.

found on the Irish crosses, the floriated sceptre being absent.
The page of the MS. is divided into four rectangular panels,

Fig. 49.—Miniature of Christ in Glory, from the St. Gall Gospels.

three of which occupy the upper half of the page, and the
fourth fills the lower half. In the centre panel, at the top, is
Christ, with the nimbus round the head, holding a book in His

left hand, and raising the right in the attitude of giving the benediction. A cross, inclined diagonally, is supported between the
arm and the body. In the panels on each side are nimbed
angels blowing trumpets, and in the lower panel are twelve
figures holding books and gazing upwards, possibly intended for
the Apostles.

In the Saxon MSS. of the same period the subject of Christ
in Glory is not an uncommon one, the most interesting example
perhaps being in the Saxon Psalter of King Athelstan, of the
tenth century, in the British Museum (Galba A. xviii).[1] There
are three miniatures in the volume, one of the Ascension, and
the other two of Christ in Glory. The first is inscribed ASCENSIO
DNI. The Saviour is enthroned, holding a book, and enclosed
within an oval aureole, supported by four angels, with the
Virgin (MARIA) and the men of Galilee (VIRI GALILEI). In the
next miniature Christ is enthroned, holding the cross, having the
letters Alpha and Omega on each side, and enclosed within a
vesica-shaped aureole, around which are the Choir of Martyrs
(OMNIS CHORUS MARTYRUM), the Choir of Confessors (OMNIS CHORUS
CONFESSORUM), and the Choir of Virgins (OMNIS CHORUS VIRGINUM).
In the four corners are angels. The third miniature shows our
Lord enthroned, holding a book, with the cross, spear, and sponge,
emblems of the Passion, at each side, and enclosed within a
vesica-shaped aureole. Around and below are the Choir of
Angels (OMNIS CHORUS ANGELORUM), the Choir of Prophets
(OMNIS CHORUS PROPHETARUM), the Virgin Mary, St. Peter, with
the monogrammatic key, St. Paul, and the other Apostles.

In the Greek Painter's Guide from Mount Athos,[2] it is specified that the saints who go to meet Christ at His Second Coming
shall be divided into nine choirs, and those present at the Last
Judgment into three choirs, in the following order—Apostles,
First Parents, Patriarchs, Prophets, Bishops, Martyrs, Saints,
Righteous Kings, and Holy Women. It is possible, therefore,
that the two miniatures in the Athelstan Psalter may be intended for the Second Advent. Strictly speaking, the representations of Christ in Glory should be purely symbolical, and
no figures introduced except the angels supporting the aureole
on the evangelistic beasts.

---

[1] Westwood's *Miniatures*, pl. 32.

[2] Didron's *Christian Iconography*, by Miss Stokes, vol. ii, p. 345.

It will be seen that the chief difference between the Irish and the Saxon treatment of the subject of Christ in Glory is, that in the latter case the figure of the Saviour is surrounded by an aureole, a feature which we shall find subsequently in Norman sculpture. An aureole is a glory applied to the whole body, in the same way that the nimbus is to the head, but its use is more restricted; for whereas the nimbus was given indiscriminately to both Scriptural personages and also to Saints, the aureole is only an attribute of the three Persons of the Trinity, the Virgin Mary, and the Soul.[1] Probably one of the earliest instances of the aureole round the figure of the Saviour is to be found in the miniature of the Ascension, in the Syriac Gospels of Rabula (A.D. 586), in the Medicean Library at Florence,[2] before mentioned. The aureole may possibly have been developed out of the rectangular and circular frames, enclosing a cross or bust of Christ, supported by angels at each side, which occur upon the sculptured sarcophagi at Rome and elsewhere.[3] The aureole is quite unknown in Irish art, and the nimbus is but sparingly used. It is difficult to assign a reason for the absence of the nimbus round the heads of sacred personages upon most of the Celtic sculptured stones, and in some of the MSS., as the way of treating many of the subjects shows that they must have been copied from Byzantine originals, and in these the nimbus is always present.

Upon most of the pre-Norman sculptured stones of the ancient kingdom of Northumbria we find the nimbus, but the only example which exists in the purely Celtic area of Great Britain is upon the cross of King Fland at Clonmacnois.[4] In the Saxon and Hiberno-Saxon MSS. the nimbus is never absent; but in the Irish MSS. it is either wholly omitted, or placed round some of the heads and not round others.[5] The leaving out of

[1] Miss Twining's *Christian Symbols and Emblems*, pls. 33, 34, 71, 92. On pl. 80 is a figure of the Devil cast down into hell, within a vesica, copied from the twelfth century MS. in the Brit. Mus. (Claud. B. iv).

[2] R. St. John Tyrwhitt's *Art Teaching of the Primitive Church*, p. 306, copied from Assemani's *Catalogue of the Medicean Library*.

[3] Martigny's *Dict.*, p. 257.

[4] O'Neill's *Irish Crosses*, pl. 23.

[5] As in the *Book of Kells*, where, in the miniature of the Virgin and Child, the former is nimbed, whilst the latter is not ; and in the Gospels

the nimbus upon the sculptured stones is one of the chief causes which renders the interprētation of the subjects so difficult.

The figure of Christ within an aureole occurs in five different scenes, which must not be confounded with each other, namely, the Transfiguration, the Ascension, Christ in Glory, the Second Advent, and the Last Judgment. They may be easily discriminated by the attitude of the Saviour's hands, the objects He carries, and the surrounding figures. In the Transfiguration Christ is surrounded by an aureole with eight rays like the spokes of a wheel; on each side are Moses and Elias; below are the three disciples, Peter, James, and John; and above the head of the Saviour, the Dextera Dei.[1] In the Ascension, Christ carries the cross of the Resurrection, and stretches forth His hand towards the Dextera Dei, issuing from a cloud, the aureole being placed diagonally; below are the Virgin Mary and the Disciples.[2] Christ in Glory is seated on a throne, gives the benediction with the right hand, and holds a book in the left. In this case there are no accessories, except the symbols of the four Evangelists or angels supporting the aureole.

The Last Judgment is the most important subject that comes within the whole range of Christian art, both as being the final scene, for which the preceding ones are but a preparation, and on account of the scope it offers for the display of the imaginative faculty in grouping together all the actors in the great drama of life, and introducing those weird surroundings which make the mediæval conceptions of the Doom so terrible. Tertullian calls the last and eternal judgment the greatest spectacle of all; but notwithstanding this there is nothing in the paintings of the Catacombs at Rome during the first four centuries to show that the early Christians ever dwelt on the idea of

of MacDurnan, where St. Matthew is nimbed, but St. Luke is not. The symbols of the four Evangelists are nimbed in the Stockholm and Lindisfarne Gospels, but not in the Books of Kells, Durrow, Treves, St. Chad, and the Paris Gospels. The nimbus is to be found in the Gospels of Stockholm, Kells, Lindisfarne, St. Gall, St. Chad, MacDurnan, Treves; Psalter, Brit. Mus. (Vesp. A. i), Cassiodorus on the Psalms, Durham. (See Westwood's *Miniatures*.)

[1] See Carlovingian Ivories in the South Kensington Museum. (Maskell, *Catal.*)

[2] In the Æthelwold Benedictional. (*Archæologia*, vol. xxiv.)

Christ as the stern judge dealing out rewards to the good and avenging Himself-on the wicked, or, indeed, that they believed in a place of future punishment at all.

When the classical traditions which influenced the art of the Catacombs died out, all sense of beauty and belief in the loving characteristics of the Saviour disappeared with them, and in place of the Good Shepherd carrying the lost sheep tenderly on His shoulders back to the fold, the Byzantine mosaics represent Christ majestic, but stern and devoid of pity. The awe-inspiring appearance given to the Saviour in Byzantine art was retained in the sculptures of the Last Judgment of the eleventh and twelfth centuries, which are to be seen on the west fronts of many of the foreign cathedrals ; but other details, such as the tortures of the damned, are traceable to the vivid Northern imagination at the time when Christianity was being engrafted upon Teutonic paganism. One of the earliest and most interesting examples of the Last Judgment is the sculpture over the west doorway of Autun Cathedral, in France, executed by Gislebert, probably in the eleventh century.[1]

In the Latin Church this subject is usually sculptured upon the west wall outside, and in the Greek Church it is painted on the west wall inside. In England, paintings of the Doom over the chancel-arch are not uncommon, but they are mostly of late date. There is, however, one of the twelfth century still remaining at Chaldon in Surrey.[2]

In MSS. before the twelfth century pictures of the Last Judgment occur but seldom.

The conception of the scene is founded upon the descriptions given in Daniel (ch. vii), St. Matthew (ch. xxiv), and in the Revelations (ch. xx), supplemented by texts from other parts of both the Old and New Testaments. A complete representation comprises the following features. In the centre the Second Person of the Trinity, not the First, as Judge, according to our Lord's own words (John v, 22) and the testimony of the Apostles (Acts x, 42), enthroned (Romans xiv, 10, and 2 Cor. v, 10), and

[1] *Journ. Brit. Archœol. Inst.*, vol. xl, p. 115 ; Du Sommerard's *Les Arts du Moyen Age*, Album, 3rd Series.

[2] C. E. Keyser's *List of Buildings with Mural Paintings*, p. 354 ; *Journ. B. A. Inst.*, vol. xxx, p. 35 ; *Surrey Archœol. Coll.*, vol. v, p. 279.

surrounded by an aureole (Matt. xxiv, 30), with a rainbow across it (Rev. iv, 3), extending His hands evenly on each side to dispense equal justice to the good and evil alike. In the Greek Church, and the later examples belonging to the Latin Church, this attitude of impartiality is not found, but Christ is shown blessing the saints with the right hand, whilst He points out the place of torment to sinners with the left; or, with the wounded hand (Rev. i, 7) extended palm upwards to the good, and presenting the back to the evil. The Greek Church represents His throne like the fiery flame, and His wheels as burning fire (Daniel vii, 9).

Upon each side of Christ sit the Twelve Apostles, "upon twelve thrones, judging the twelve tribes of Israel" (Matt. xx, 28), and the Virgin Mary and John the Baptist,[1] in illustration of St. Paul's words, "Do ye not know that the Saints shall judge the world?" (1 Cor. vi, 2). With them, upon the right-hand side, are also the good, holding branches in their hands, symbolical of their virtues. They are distributed in three orders: first, the Choir of First Parents, Patriarchs, and Prophets; secondly, the Choir of Bishops, Martyrs, and Hermits; and thirdly, the Choir of Holy Kings, Women, and Martyrs. On the left hand of Christ are all sinners driven from His presence, and condemned with the devils and the traitor Judas. The sorrows and tortures of the damned by demons are shown in a variety of horrible ways. Angels are seen blowing trumpets (1 Thes. iv, 16, and 1 Cor. xv, 52), and gathering together His elect from the four winds, from one end of heaven to the other (Matt. xxiv, 31). Other angels, for which there is no Scriptural warrant, hold emblems of the Passion, or help St. Michael to weigh the souls, and deliver the good ones to the gates of the heavenly Jerusalem.

The scene of the Last Judgment is generally combined with that of the Resurrection from the Dead, which is placed below, forming a horizontal band extending the whole breadth of the picture. According to the Latin Church the bodies are shown rising out of stone coffins, or sometimes from simple graves dug in the ground, the good being on the right hand of Christ the Judge, and the wicked on His left, with an

---

[1] Or, in the thirteenth century, St. John the Evangelist with the Virgin kneeling and offering up supplications for the Holy Church.

N

angel in the centre holding a drawn sword separating the two, in the words of the Prophet Daniel (xii, 2), "And many of them that sleep in the dust of the earth shall awake, some to everlasting life, and some to shame and everlasting contempt."

The Greek Church represents the scene differently, and instead of the bodies coming out of holes in the earth they are shown being disgorged by sea-monsters and other beasts, following the text in the Revelations (xx, 13), "And the sea gave up the dead that were in it; and death and hell delivered up the dead which were in them; and they were judged every man according to their works." In a subsequent lecture we shall see the importance of this passage, as explaining the figures of animals throwing portions of human beings out of their mouths, which occur on the Scotch crosses and in Norman sculpture. The Greek Church also includes, in the picture, an angel folding up a mighty scroll, on which is to be seen the sun, moon, and stars, in illustration of the verse in the Revelations (vi, 14), "And the heaven departed as a scroll when it is rolled together."

Having reviewed the leading features in the scene of the Last Judgment, we are now in a position to examine more critically the peculiarities exhibited in the representation of the subject on the cross of Muiredach at Monasterboice. It should be noticed that some of the deviations from the conventional type are due to the shape of that part of the cross which has been chosen by the sculptor for his design, necessitating undue crowding together, or omission of figures where the space becomes restricted by the hollows at the intersections of the arms. I think this accounts for there being only a single enthroned figure on the Saviour's left hand, where usually we see the Twelve Apostles, the Virgin Mary, and St. John. There is no room for a well-balanced composition, as on the tympanum at Autun Cathedral, where every detail on the right has one to correspond with it on the left—Christ in the centre, the four angels blowing trumpets at the four corners, Sol on one side, Luna on the other, the gates of the heavenly Jerusalem contrasting with the Mouth of Hell; St. Peter with key of Heaven being placed in opposition to St. Michael weighing souls, the good with angels on the right of Christ, and the wicked with devils on His left. On the cross of Muiredach, in front of our Lord, on His right, is a kneeling figure, with an open book above the head. The book is described in the Revelations (xx, 12), "And I saw the dead, small and great, stand before God ; and the books were opened : and another book was opened ; which is the book of life : and the dead were judged out of those things which were written in the books, according to their works." (See also Daniel vii, 10, and xii, 1.) The kneeling figure is probably the soul being judged. In some Byzantine Last Judgments we see an altar, with the book of justice, the cross, and other emblems of the Passion upon it, on each side of which kneel Adam and Eve.[1] David playing on the harp and leading the heavenly choir, on the right of the Saviour, in contrast to the souls of the wicked being driven from His presence by a devil with a three-pronged fork, has already been mentioned.

St. Michael weighing the Souls.

The only remaining subject to be considered is that of St. Michael weighing the Souls, which is placed immediately below the feet of our Lord. There are three figures in the composition. St. Michael is of gigantic stature, holding a staff with one hand and weighing a small human being in the pan of the scales nearest to him : a prostrate devil below is pushing up the light pan of the scale. The balance is suspended by a chain to a cross-bar above. On the wall-painting at Chaldon, in Surrey, St. Michael holds up the scales ; and on the Autun tympanum this office is performed by the hand of the Almighty issuing from a cloud. The weighing of the souls is not strictly speaking a Scriptural subject, although it may have been suggested by texts in the Bible. Michael is mentioned in only three of the books of Scripture : in Daniel (x, 13), where he is

---

[1] Didron, *Guide de la Peinture*, p. 270. The inscriptions are—for Adam, "Adam per crucem redemptus, crucem adorat", and a similar one for Eve ; for the Cross, " Quæ crux ita radiat quod splendorem solis et lunæ sua claritate obscurat"; for the book, "Liber justiciæ sunt exempla sanctorum, qui aperietur in præsentia Dei, quia tunc aperte scient mali se non prædestinatos ad vitam. Liber Vitæ est Christus, qui suis dabit vitam."

described as one of the chief princes ; in Jude (9), as the Archangel contending with the devil, and disputing about the body of Moses; and in the Revelation (xii, 7) as fighting with his angels against the dragon.

Michael, Prince of Persia, seems to have been confused with Michael the Archangel, and the text which connects him with the Last Judgment is that in Daniel (xii, 1), which says: "And at that time shall Michael stand up, the great prince, which standeth for the children of thy people; and there shall be a time of trouble . . . . and at that time thy people shall be delivered,

Fig. 50.—St. Michael weighing souls on end of sculptured slab of fourteenth century in Kildare Cathedral.

every one that shall be found written in the book." Balances are mentioned in Daniel (v, 27), "Thou art tried in the balance and found wanting"; and also in the Revelation (vi, 5), "And I beheld, and lo a black horse; and he that sat on him had a pair of balances in his hand"; but there is nothing to connect St. Michael with the operation of weighing, which fell to his lot as being chief of the angels and guardian of souls.

Everyone who has studied Egyptian antiquities must have been struck with the marked similarity between the Christian representations of the weighing of souls and the pagan treatment of the same subject, as found on the wall-paintings in the tombs of Egypt, where Osiris, the Judge of the Dead, is seen on a throne, attended by Isis and Nepthys looking on, whilst Anubis stands on one side of a pair of balances, in which a soul is being weighed against an image of the God of Truth, whilst Thoth stands at the other recording the judgment on a tablet.[1] By a curious coincidence the two symbols of office are held by Osiris exactly in the same way that the cross and sceptre are held by Christ upon the Irish crosses. For further information on this subject, consult Didron's *Christian Iconography*, edited by Miss Stokes, vol. ii, chapter on the " Iconography of the Soul".

St. Michael weighing the souls is not an uncommon subject in the twelfth century sculpture in France, there being good examples on capitals of columns at the church of St. Croix, at St. Lô in Normandy (*Mém. de la Soc. des Ant. de la Normandie —Atlas*); at the church of St. Pierre, at Chauvigny, near Poitiers (De Caumont, *Bulletin Monumental*, vol. ix); at Montivilliers, near Havre (*Revue de l'Art Chrét.*, vol. v); and at Illats, in Gironde (*Revue de l'Art Chrét.*, vol vii). L'Abbé Crosnier gives some interesting details about the treatment of the Last Judgment in early art, in his *Iconographic Chrétienne*, and describes the capital of a column at St. Révérien, in the diocese of Nevers, upon which the soul to be weighed is not placed in a balance, but on a flat plate held by the Dextera Dei. The Last Judgments on the Greek wall paintings at Salamis and in the twelfth century MS. of the *Hortus Deliciarum* of Herrad, formerly existing at Strasbourg, are fully discussed in Didron's *Guide de la Peinture.*

[1] Sir G. Wilkinson's *Ancient Egyptians*, vol. iii, p. 468.

LECTURE IV.

THE HIGH CROSSES OF IRELAND,—SUBJECTS ON THE SHAFTS AND BASES.

THE name of M. Didron is, or should be, familiar to every student of Christian iconography. When the great French *savant* visited Greece in 1839 he was particularly struck by the stereotyped form of Eastern art as compared with Western. In the pictures and sculptures of the Latin Church, although ancient traditions are followed in the general treatment of the subject, a certain amount of freedom is allowed to the individual. In the Greek Church this is not the case. To use M. Didron's own words : "The artist is the slave of the theologian; his work, which is copied by his successors, is in turn inspired by the painters who have preceded him. The Greek artist is enslaved by tradition, as the animal is guided by instinct; he draws a figure as the swallow builds its nest, or as the bee makes its comb. He is master of execution; the art is his, but the art alone; because the conception and the idea belong to the Fathers, the theologians, and the Catholic Church."[1]

M. Didron made it his business to find out how it was that the decorators of the churches were able to repeat the same figures and inscriptions, generation after generation, even when, as at Salamis, they are numbered by the thousand, without ever deviating from the prescribed copies. The mystery was solved when he arrived at Mount Athos,[2] and, ascending the scaffold, he found the painter surrounded by his pupils, engaged in orna-

---

[1] *Manuel d'Iconographie Chrétienne*, p. ix.

[2] For descriptions of the Monasteries of Mount Athos, see R. Curzon's *Monasteries of the Levant*, and Didron's *Annales Archéologiques*, vol. v, p. 148.

menting the narthex of the church with frescoes. The master rapidly sketched the outlines of the figures entirely from memory, without ever making a mistake, stopping now and then to dictate long sentences to his pupils, which were to be inscribed on the pictures.

On M. Didron's expressing his astonishment at the skill and prodigious effort of memory involved in the process, the artist replied, "But, sir, all this is much less wonderful than you suppose, for see here is a MS. which tells us all we ought to do. Here we are taught to prepare our plaster, our brushes, our colours, to compose and arrange our pictures; there also are written the inscriptions and sentences which we have to paint, and which you heard me dictate to these young pupils of mine."

The MS. in question is a sixteenth century copy of an original supposed to have been compiled by Dionisius the monk, painter to the convent of Fourna, near Agrapha, who had studied the famous paintings of Panselinos. Additions have been made from time to time, but it is still in use as the manual of fresco painting in the churches of Greece.[1] M. Didron had a careful copy made of this MS., which he presented to the King of Bavaria. It has been translated into French by M. Paul Durand, and published with notes by M. Didron in 1845, under the title of *Manuel d'Iconographie Chrétienne Greque et Latine.* The title of the original MS. is, Ἑρμηνεία τῆς ζωγραφικῆς, or Guide to Painting. It deserves careful study from every student of Christian antiquities. The book is divided into three parts; the first dealing with the methods of preparing the materials required for painting; the second giving detailed descriptions of how all the subjects are to be treated, and what inscriptions are to be added; and the third specifying the appropriate arrangement of the pictures as regards their position on the walls of the church.[2]

The latter question, although one of very great importance, has not received the attention it deserves from archæologists. Perhaps the reason of this is that we possess no complete series of frescoes or sculptures to show what scheme of arrangement

---

[1] R. Curzon's *Monasteries of the Levant,* p. 17.

[2] A translation of the *Painter's Guide* will be found in Didron's *Christian Iconography,* edited by Miss Stokes, vol. ii.

was generally followed. The practice of placing pictures of sacred subjects in a definite relation one to another began in the Catacombs at Rome. Here the surface to be decorated was usually a hemispherical dome, in the centre of which was placed the principal subject, with others in radial compartments surrounding it. Both Old and New Testament types were used together, without any marked distinction being made between them; and as nearly all the types were of about equal importance, there was no necessity for arranging them in an ascending or descending series. Historical sequence was also neglected. On the sculptured sarcophagi, owing to the difference of the shape of the surface to be decorated, the subjects were placed on each side of a centre instead of round it. With this new arrangement we find the idea of antithesis introduced, the Old Testament types being placed on one side of the centre and the New Testament types on the other. In the mosaics of the Basilicas we have another form of surface, namely, the half-dome, which gave an opportunity of placing the principal subject, which was generally Christ in Glory, at the top, and the Angels, Apostles, Prophets, Saints, and Martyrs in order of precedence one below the other, whilst the Old and New Testament types were still separated, one on each side of the central axis. Besides the relation of the subjects to each other, when the ritual of the Church became more advanced, particular scenes were painted on those portions of the sacred edifice to which they were deemed most appropriate, so that the nave, chancel, transepts, east end, west end, baptistery, doorways, etc., each had their own special set of subjects.

The shapes of spaces to be decorated may be classified as rectangles, triangles, circles, and semicircles, corresponding on rounded surfaces to cylinders, spherical triangles, domes, and apsidal or half-domes. The other considerations to be taken into account are symmetry, with regard to a certain point or line, and order of sequence. In all systems of decoration the most important subject is placed in the centre, and the others are made to lead up to it, the contrast being effected by arranging the opposite elements, such as good and evil, type and anti-type, men and women, Jews and Gentiles, on each side of the axis of symmetry.

The most complete scheme of decoration of an ecclesiastical building is probably to be found at Chartres Cathedral in France; and in this country the west front of Wells Cathedral is a very fine example of symbolic sculpture.

The earliest description which has been preserved of the scheme of decoration of an English church is to be found in the Venerable Bede's *Lives of the Holy Abbots*.[1] From this source we learn that Benedict Biscop, returning from Gaul A.D. 675, after his third voyage to Rome, "brought with him pictures of sacred representations to adorn the Church of St. Peter,[2] which he had built, namely, a likeness of the Virgin Mary and of the Twelve Apostles, with which he intended to adorn the central nave, on boarding placed from one wall to the other; also some figures from Gospel history for the south wall, and others from the Revelation of St. John for the north wall; so that everyone who entered the church, even if they could not read, whenever they turned their eyes might have before them the loving countenance of Christ and His Saints, though it were but in a picture, and with watchful minds might meditate upon the benefits of the Lord's Incarnation, and having before their eyes the perils of the Last Judgment, might examine their hearts more strictly on that account."

No such paintings have survived the destructive ravages of time, but we have on the high crosses of Ireland a complete scheme of decorative Christian sculpture as applied to monuments. In the last lecture we examined those subjects which were chosen, from their importance, to occupy the most prominent positions; on the present occasion we shall study the scenes which lead up to them. The principal subjects, the Crucifixion and Christ in Glory, are placed in the centre of the cross; the others are enclosed within panels on the shafts.

The Temptation of Adam and Eve.

On the cross of Muiredach at Monasterboice, on the lowest compartment of the shafts on the same side which bears the representation of the Last Judgment, described in the previous

[1] A. Giles' edition, vol. iv, p. 369.
[2] Monkwearmouth, founded A.D. 674.

lecture, we find a sculpture of the Temptation and Expulsion[1] of Adam and Eve. These scenes occur together on three of the other high crosses of Ireland,[2] and the Temptation by itself is to be found in seven instances.[3] In Scotland there are two crosses with the Temptation of Adam and Eve upon them,[4] but I know of no example in other parts of Great Britain on sculptured stones of the pre-Norman period.

With regard to the miniatures of the MSS. the case is reversed, for although we have Saxon pictures of Adam and Eve

Fig. 51.—Temptation and Expulsion (?) of Adam and Eve on shaft of Cross of Muiredach, at Monasterboice.

in Cædmon's *Paraphrase of the Scriptures* and in Ælfric's *Heptateuch,* we have no Irish ones. The reason of this is because the scene of the Fall of our First Parents illustrates the third chapter of Genesis, and no illuminated Irish MSS. of the Old

---

[1] Dr. J. Anderson suggests that the second scene is not the Expulsion, but the Murder of Abel, and the weapon held in the hand of one of the figures is certainly more like a club than the sword which the angel should carry.

[2] At Monasterboice, and two crosses at Kells.

[3] At Kells, Arboe, Moone Abbey, Drumcliff, Tynan, and two crosses at Castle Dermot.

[4] At Farnell and Iona.

Testament have survived to the present day.   It will therefore
be seen of what very great importance the sculptured stones are
in supplementing our knowledge of early Christian symbolism
in this country, and it is fervently to be hoped that an effort
will be made to preserve some record of the designs by means
of photographs and casts, before the destructive effect of weather-
ing has removed every trace.

How long will it be before it is recognised that the scientific
value of the results obtained from the study of the sculptured
stones is in no way inferior to that derived from the miniatures
of the MSS ?   Yet it is curious to note the difference between
the means taken to preserve the one and the other.   In our
great libraries no one is allowed to examine the more important
MSS., except under special conditions, which preclude the possibility of their being injured ; but if anyone wishes to immortalise
himself by cutting his name upon one of the early Christian
monuments of this country, or feels inclined to break off a piece
to carry away as a memento, I know of nothing to prevent his
doing so.   It is difficult to find words to express the folly of
allowing such priceless treasures to decay year after year,
without the slightest effort being made either to place them
under cover, beyond the reach of the hand of the spoiler, or to
take copies which may survive to be handed down to posterity,
when the stones themselves no longer exist.   However, the
good work must not be further delayed, or it will be too late,
for in a few years there will be nothing remaining to show that
we once possessed a national school of Christian art, of which,
if it had existed in any other country but our own, we should
have been the first to recognise the value.

But to return to the subject of Adam and Eve.   The position
chosen for the scene on the Irish crosses is usually at the base
of the shaft, although in two cases it occurs at the top.   The
Fall of Adam is the first and most important of all the Old
Testament types which have reference to the doctrines of
Christianity.   It was the Fall of Adam which rendered the
Atonement necessary, and the symbolism is made clear in the
beautiful chapter on the Resurrection in St. Paul's Epistle to
the Corinthians (1 Cor. xv, 21), containing the verse, " For as in
Adam all die, even so in Christ shall all be made alive."   The

representations of Adam and Eve were also looked upon by the early Church as refuting the errors of the Gnostics, and showing that the creation of man was the work of God and not of the evil principle.[1] No scene is found so universally throughout the whole range of Christian art from the earliest times down to the present day, and in none have the conventional features varied less.

Fig. 52.—Temptation of Adam and Eve on broken cross shaft in Kells Churchyard.

The first dated example is to be seen on the sarcophagus of Junius Bassus at St. Peter's in Rome (A.D. 359).   In the centre is a tree with leaves like those of an oak, round the trunk of which the serpent is coiled, his head looking towards Eve, who stands on the right.   On the left is Adam, who, like Eve, hides his nakedness with a large fig-leaf, quite out of proportion with the leaves of the tree in the centre.   A sheaf of corn stands next Adam and a sheep next Eve, typical of the labours which they had to undergo in order to make the earth bring forth its fruit after the Fall.   It will be noticed that here, as in many

[1] Martigny's *Dict.*, p. 19.

other representations where symbolism is the point of greatest importance, historical accuracy is found wanting. The Bible distinctly says, that at the time of the Temptation "they were both naked, the man and his wife, and were not ashamed" (Gen. ii, 25). It was not until they had eaten the fruit of the tree that "the eyes of both of them were opened, and they knew that they were naked; and they sewed fig-leaves together and made themselves aprons" (Gen. iii, 7). However, the inaccuracy of the representations consists not in perverting the words of Scripture so much as in crowding several incidents into one, and

Fig. 53.—Temptation of Adam and Eve on shaft of Cross at Iona.

making them take place simultaneously, instead of one after another. We have remarked upon the same thing in the case of the soldiers bearing the sponge and spear at the Crucifixion.

The representations of the Fall of our First Parents may be divided into three classes—(1) where historical accuracy is adhered to, and neither Adam nor Eve evince any feelings of shame, but are entirely engaged in the act of receiving the apple from the serpent and handing it from one to the other. The number of apples varies according to whether one action only is shown, or whether the artist saw fit to make the three consecutive actions —Eve receiving the apple from the serpent, Eve handing it to

Adam, and Adam eating it—all take place at once. This form is the least common in early art. (2) Where Adam and Eve are receiving or presenting the apple with one hand and hiding their nakedness with the other. This form is most common in Norman sculpture.[1] (3) Where Adam and Eve are covering their nakedness with both hands. This is the form which occurs most frequently on the sculptured sarcophagi at Rome and on the Irish high crosses. Throughout all periods of Christian art Eve is generally shown on the right side of the tree and Adam on the left; but the rule is not always adhered to.

The special features which characterise the Celtic representations of the Temptation are the exaggeration of the crossing of the hands, in order to indicate an attitude of shame, and the peculiar way in which the branches of the tree are made to form an arch enclosing the figures on each side. Instead of leaves on the boughs, there are a quantity of round berries, each on a single stem. The kind of tree is not specified in the Bible, but as in the seventh verse of the third chapter of Genesis, immediately following the one describing the Fall, it says that Adam and Eve sewed fig-leaves together to make themselves aprons, the Greek Church has assumed that the tree of knowledge was a fig-tree. The species varies according to the locality, the apple being most common in the art of the Latin Church. Sometimes, however, the orange, vine, and cherry are seen.[2] On sculptured Norman fonts at Cotham and Cowlam in Yorkshire, and at East Meon in Hants, the tree is shown with branches much interlaced, as is common in the art of the period. In the mediæval bestiaries,[3] and in the Biblia Pauperum,[4] the upper part of the figure of the Almighty, as Christ with the cruciferous nimbus, is shown in the midst of the foliage of the Tree of Knowledge, probably in reference to the verse in Genesis (iii, 8), "And they heard the voice of the Lord God, walking in the

---

[1] Occasionally two and three are combined. Adam hides his nakedness with both hands, whilst Eve hides hers with only one. (Garrucci, Storia del Arte Cristiana, vol. vi, pl. 312, and vice versâ, vol. vi, pl. 376.

[2] Didron, Guide de la Peinture, p. 80.

[3] Cahier and Martin, Mélanges d'Archéologie, vol. iii, p. 284: "We place the Saviour in this tree (Arbor Perindex) because He is the lignum vitæ of all who believe on Him."

[4] J. P. Berjeau's reprint.

garden in the cool of the evening." The companion picture in
the *Biblia Pauperum* is the Creator appearing to Moses out
of the burning bush, which scene is treated in a similar manner.
There are some curious legends connecting the Tree of Knowledge with the cross.[1]

In rare instances we find the tree placed at one side instead
of in the centre, as on a sculptured sarcophagus given by

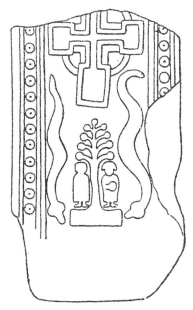

Fig. 54.—Temptation of Adam and Eve on sculptured stone at Farnell.

Garrucci,[2] and in Ælfric's *Anglo-Saxon Heptateuch*.[3] On the
cross-slab from Farnell in Forfarshire, now in the Montrose
Museum, there are two serpents introduced into the scene of
the Fall, one at each side, with Adam and Eve standing by the
tree in the centre. The serpent is, in later times, from the
thirteenth century onwards, given the head of a woman, and this

---

[1] In the miniature of the Crucifixion in the Saxon Psalter in the Cambridge University Library, the word "Lignum Vitæ" is inscribed on the
cross.

[2] *Storia del Arte Cristiana*, vol. v, pl. 374.

[3] Brit. Mus. (Claud. B. iv), eleventh century. (See T. Wright's *Hist.
of Caricature and Grotesque*, p. 57.)

receives sanction from the writings of Bede, who tells us Lucifer chose the species of serpent which had a female head, because " like are attracted to like".[1]

There are some remarkable sculptures of the Fall on the capital of one of the columns of the Cathedral at Iona,[2] which, although executed in the fourteenth century, preserves all the

Fig. 55.—Temptation of Adam and Eve on eighteenth century tombstone at Logierait.

archaic features of the Irish crosses. Even in the eighteenth century the ancient symbolic treatment of this subject still survived upon tombstones in remote village churchyards, as at Logierait in Perthshire,[3] where Adam and Eve with aprons of fig-leaves sewn together to hide their nakedness, instead of the large cabbage-life leaf seen in the earlier representations, are

[1] Mrs. Jameson's *Life of Our Lord*, vol. i, p. 100.

[2] H. D. Graham's *Antiquities of Iona*, pl. 41.

[3] Other tombstones with Adam and Eve exist at Falkirk, Little Dunkeld, and Uphall, in Scotland, and at St. John Leonard, Gloucestershire.

placed under an arch, round which is inscribed, "The serpent deceived Eve". The whole of the story of the Fall, as told in the third chapter of Genesis, is generally compressed into one scene, with the exception of the Expulsion from Paradise, which is treated separately. On three of the Irish crosses we have the

Fig. 56.—Temptation of Adam and Eve, on Font at Cotham. *From a rubbing by the Rev. G. F. Browne.*

Temptation and Expulsion side by side, enclosed in the same panel. On the sculptured sarcophagi at Rome the curse pronounced by God against Adam and Eve is symbolised by a sheaf of corn and a sheep, either placed beside[1] them or being

[1] Garrucci, *Storia del Arte Cristiana*, vol. v, pls. 314, 365, 366.

presented to them by God.[1] In the Saxon MSS.[2] and on Norman fonts[3] the same idea is indicated by an angel, who gives a spade to Adam and a spindle and distaff to Eve. Apart from the symbolism of these representations, the ancient forms of agricultural implements and spinning apparatus exhibited are of the greatest interest. The Saxon spade is of the same one-sided

Fig. 57.—Temptation of Adam and Eve, on Font at Cowlam. (*From a rubbing by the Rev. G. F. Browne.*)

shape as those still in use in the Western Islands of Scotland, of which specimens may be seen in the Edinburgh Museum of Antiquities. The only two Saxon MSS. in existence containing

[1] Garrucci, *Storia del Arte Cristiana*, pl. 381.

[2] Ælfric's *Heptateuch*, B. M. (Claud. B. iv), twelfth century MS., B. M. (Nero C. iv).

[3] East Meon, Hants ; Hook Norton, Oxon.

pictures illustrative of the earlier books of the Old Testament
are the *Heptateuch* of Ælfric, Archbishop of Canterbury, who died
A.D. 1066, in the British Museum (Claud. B. iv) ; and the metrical
Paraphrase of the Scriptures of Cædmon, in the Bodleian
Library at Oxford (Junius, No. 11), written in about the
eleventh century. Both of these MSS. contain drawings of the
Temptation and Expulsion of Adam and Eve. The whole of
those in Cædmon's *Paraphrase of the Scriptures* have been
engraved in the *Archæologia*,[1] and the text has been published
by Thorpe.[2] A verbal description would in no way do justice
to this most wonderful series of illustrations of Anglo-Saxon art,
and I cannot therefore too strongly recommend a careful study
of the book itself, a thorough knowledge of which is absolutely
essential to a comprehension of the Christian symbolism of the
period. In the series given in Cædmon's *Paraphrase* the
diffuseness with which the subject is treated forms a very
marked contrast to the representations on the Irish crosses,
where, symbolism being the chief object, as many different
actions as possible are compressed into one.

Side by side with the scenes described as having taken place
in the Bible, we are shown their connection with the contest
going on between the powers of good and evil in the spiritual
world.

The Adoration of the Magi.

The subject occupying the top panel of the shaft of the cross
of Muiredach at Monasterboice, on the same side as the
Temptation of Adam and Eve, appears to be the Adoration of
the Magi. The Virgin Mary is shown seated on the throne,
holding the infant Saviour in her arms ; in front are the three
wise men, with a fourth figure behind, and above the head of
Christ is the star. The Adoration of the Magi is not found on
the paintings in the Catacombs[3] at Rome until the end of the
third century, but upon the sculptured sarcophagi[4] it is one of
the scenes most frequently represented. It occurs also upon the

[1] Vol. xxiv.
[2] Benjamin Thorpe. London, 1832.
[3] Northcote and Brownlow's *Roma Sotterranea*, vol. ii, p. 169.
[4] *Ibid.*, vol. ii, p. 262. On eleven out of fifty sarcophagi in the Lateran
Museum at Rome.

sculptured details of Italian churches[1] in the eighth century, upon Norman fonts[2] in England, and its popularity lasted down to a late period. I can find no example of it in the Irish MSS., and only two in Saxon MSS., the Missal of Archbishop Robert of Canterbury in the Public Library at Rouen,[3] and in the Benedictional of Æthelwold in the Library of the Duke of Devonshire.[4] Besides being an event in the history of our Lord, the Adoration of the Magi was used by the early Church to symbolise the belief in the divinity of Christ and the Virgin

Fig. 58.—Adoration of the Magi, on shaft of Cross of Muiredach at Monasterboice.

Mary, and also to typify the conversion of the Gentiles to Christianity.

The traditional number of the wise men is three, probably because St. Matthew (ii, 11) mentions three kinds of offerings, —" And when they had opened their treasures, they presented unto him gifts; gold and frankincense, and myrrh." This number is, however, considerably varied in the Catacomb paintings and elsewhere, chiefly for the sake of symmetry, the Virgin

---

[1] On the altar of Rachtis, at Cividale in Frioul. (Garrucci, *Storia del Arte Cristiana*, vol. vi, pl. 424.)

[2] Sculthorpe, Norfolk ; Cowlam, Yorkshire.

[3] Westwood's *Miniatures*, p. 136.

[4] *Archæologia*, vol. xxiv.

and Child being placed in the centre, and either one or two wise men on each side. The names given to the Magi by tradition are Gaspar, Melchior, and Balthasar. On the sculptured sarcophagi their dress consists of a short tunic, a cloak falling in long folds behind from the shoulders, and bandaged leggings. A direct connection may be traced between the Three Children in the Fiery Furnace and the Three Magi. Both are shown wearing the same kind of head-gear; and Martigny[1] gives three examples of sarcophagi on which a star is placed over the

Fig. 59.—Adoration of the Magi, on Font at Cowlam. *(From a rubbing by the Rev. G. F. Browne.)*

Three Children. St. Matthew (ii, 1) simply tells us that the wise men came from the East to Jerusalem; but in the apocryphal Gospel of the Infancy of Jesus Christ (iii, 1) it is added that their coming was prophesied by Zoroaster; and (iii, 6) we also learn that they were fire-worshippers, thus pointing to Persia as their native country. According to the Greek Church, the three wise men were kings, and they are thus represented in the art of the Western Church after about the eleventh century.

[1] *Dict. des Ant. Chrét.*, art. "Hébreux", p. 338, in the Vatican, at Milan, and St. Gilles.

Sometimes the Magi are on horseback, and the *Greek Painter's Guide from Mount Athos*[1] directs that outside the cave, described in the apocryphal Gospel of the Infancy (i, 6) as the place where Christ was born, a young man holding three horses by the bridle shall be shown, and that in the distance, on a mountain, the three Magi on horses, returning to their own country, being shown the way by an angel. Joseph is often represented standing behind the chair on which the Virgin is seated. In late examples the Virgin is crowned. The Saviour usually has the right hand raised in the act of giving the benediction. As regards the offerings, each of the wise men is drawn carrying a single object,—in the Catacombs, a flat dish or tray; in later times, a metal vase. In many cases the first of the Magi has a wreath or crown in his hand, as well as the vessel containing the spices.

The Adoration of the Magi is not a common subject on Celtic sculptured stones, and besides the example at Monasterboice I know of no other. However, we find the scene carved upon the Franks Casket in the British Museum, which Prof. Stephens believes to be of Northumbrian origin, and attributes to the ninth century. The learned Professor justly calls it " one of the oldest and costliest treasures of ancient English art now in existence." This precious relic was purchased in 1857 by Mr. A. W. Franks in France, and presented by him to the British Museum. Nothing is known of its previous history beyond the fact that it was obtained by the dealer, who sold it to Mr. Franks, from Auzon, Brionde, Haute Loire, France, where it was in use as a work-box.

The casket is made of the bone of a whale, which, according to the inscription on the front, was caught at Fergen-berg, or Fergen Hill, in the county of Durham. All four sides are most elaborately carved with scenes, which are described by Runic inscriptions running round the edge and forming a sort of frame to each. The stories illustrated are those of Romulus and Remus, Titus and the Jews, the Adoration of the Magi, and two others, which have not been satisfactorily explained.[2]

[1] Didron's *Guide de la Peinture*, p. 159.

[2] One is a blacksmith at work at his forge, and the other a battle-scene inscribed " Ægili", showing a king on a throne attacked in his stronghold.

Fig. 60.—Adoration of the Magi, on the Franks Casket in the British Museum.

Above the wise men is written the word " Mægi", or Magi, in
Runes. The Virgin is seated on a throne, with the infant
Saviour on her lap. His head is larger than that of the Virgin,
and is surrounded by a cruciferous nimbus. The star is indicated by a circular disc, divided by radiating lines. The three
wise men are in front carrying gifts, the first kneeling on one
knee. Between them and the throne is the figure of a bird.
The companion scene on the same side of the casket represents
a blacksmith at his forge,[1] a prostrate figure below two women
in front, and a man seizing two geese by the neck, as may also
be seen on the cross at Rossie Priory in Perthshire.[2] Prof.
Stephens sees in the blacksmith an illustration of the Scandinavian Weland, but it seems rather improbable that a Christian
and pagan should be placed in such close connection.

Christ seized by the Jews.

The cross of Muiredach at Monasterboice has upon the
bottom panel of the shaft, on the same side as the Crucifixion,
a sculpture of what is perhaps intended for Christ seized by the
Jews. It consists of a group of three figures, the centre one
being our Lord holding a staff, and on each side soldiers with
drawn swords, the one on the right grasping the Saviour by the
wrist. The beauty of the details of the drapery, which, executed with the minutest care, is specially remarkable ; and the
circular Celtic brooch for fastening the dress on the shoulder, is
also deserving of notice. There is no nimbus round the head
of Christ.

The subject was first identified by Prof. Westwood, who
recognised its meaning on account of its similarity to the
picture of Christ seized by the Jews in the *Book of Kells*,
illustrating Matthew xxvi, 30. The peculiar way in which the
soldiers grasp the wrists of the Saviour is the same in both cases.
The Seizure of Christ by the Jews belongs to the series of the
Passion, the earliest example of which occurs upon a sarcophagus

---

[1] Pictures of Tubal Cain as a smith occur in Cædmon's *Paraphrase of
the Scriptures*, in the Bodleian at Oxford, and in Ælfric's *Heptateuch* in
the British Museum. A blacksmith, associated with the Adoration of
the Magi, is to be seen on the font at Ingleton, Yorkshire.

[2] Stuart's *Sculptured Stones*, vol. ii, pl. 98.

in the Lateran Museum at Rome, of perhaps the fifth century.[1]
There is, however, a group of figures very much resembling that
on the cross at Monasterboice, especially with regard to the
attitude of the hands grasping the wrist, which is not uncom-
monly seen upon the sculptured sarcophagi of the fourth century[2] in association with Moses striking the Rock, and Peter
denying Christ. The group consists of two Jews, who may be

Fig. 61.—Christ seized by the Jews, on shaft of Cross of Muiredach at Monasterboice.

identified by the peculiar caps on their heads, arresting a man
who stands between them. The usually accepted interpretation
is that it represents St. Peter taxed with being a follower of
Christ; but Martigny[3] thinks that it is the Jews reproaching
Moses with having brought them out to die of thirst in the
wilderness. It is well known that the early Christians traced a

[1] Appell's *Monuments of Christian Art*, p. 21.
[2] On sarcophagus from St. Paul's extra Muros, now in the Lateran
Museum. (*Appell*, p. 16.)
[3] *Dict. des Ant. Chrét.*, art. "Juifs", p. 402.

resemblance between St. Peter and Moses, for upon a glass vessel from the Catacombs we see a figure striking a rock, with the name PETRVS inscribed instead of Moses.[1]

Fig. 62.—Christ seized by the Jews, from the *Book of Kells.*

The sculpture on the cross at Monasterboice differs from those on the sarcophagi, as the figures on each side are armed with swords in the former case ; and this fact, together with its similarity to the picture in the *Book of Kells,* makes it probable that the Seizure of Christ by the Jews is here represented.

[1] Martigny's *Dict.,* art. "Moïse", p. 474.

This scene is often combined with the Betrayal Kiss of Judas, as in the miniature in the Missal of Archbishop Leofric of Canterbury at Rouen,[1] previously referred to. We also find it alone on other crosses in Ireland,[2] and on the cross at Sandbach in Cheshire[3] Christ is being led away bound. Prof. Westwood[4] thinks that the man standing between two figures, having human bodies and beasts' heads, which occurs on crosses in Ireland and Wales,[5] represents the Seizure of Christ by the Jews, and refers to the verse in the Psalms (xxii, 16), " For the dogs have compassed me ; the assembly of the wicked have enclosed me ; they pierced my hands and my feet."

The subjects which have occupied our attention up to the present are those which occur upon the cross of Muiredach at Monasterboice, but there are several others on the Great Cross at the same place, which must not pass unnoticed. As regards size, this is one of the most remarkable monuments in Ireland, being 22 feet high ; but it has, unfortunately, been very much injured. It does not bear any inscription, so that there is no means of determining its exact age, but it probably belongs to the same period as the other crosses at Monasterboice, which were erected in the tenth century.

David, or Samson, and the Lion.

The shaft is divided into seven panels, and the lowest one, on the same side as Christ in Glory, contains a sculpture of David slaying the Lion. This scene is very liable to be confused with the conflict between Samson and the Lion, but in almost all cases where it occurs on Celtic stonework a sheep, a harp, or a shepherd's crook are added, showing clearly that David, and not Samson, is represented. However, the symbolism is in either case the same, and is typical of God's power to deliver the Christian from the power of evil. David is a far more important type of Christ than Samson, and the texts on which

[1] Westwood's *Miniatures*, pl. 40.

[2] Monasterboice (two crosses), Clonmacnois, Arboe.

[3] Lysons' *Magna Britannia*.

[4] *Miniatures*, p. 39.

[5] Moone Abbey, Kells, Castle Dermot, in Ireland ; and Penmon in Anglesey.

the symbolism is founded are more directly connected with the former than the latter. First, there are the words of David himself (1 Samuel xvii, 37), "The Lord that delivered me out of the paw of the lion and out of the paw of the bear, He will deliver me out of the hand of this Philistine." Then in the Psalm (xxii, 21), which is prophetic of the Crucifixion, are the words, "Save me from the lion's mouth"; and, lastly, we find St. Paul making use of the simile in the Epistle to Timothy (2 Tim. iv, 17), "Notwithstanding, the Lord stood with me and strengthened me; that by me the preaching might be fully known, and that all the Gentiles might hear; and I was

Fig. 63.—David and the Lion on Crosses—(1) in town of Kells, and (2) at Kilcullen.

delivered out of the mouth of the lion." It is curious, however, that in the *Greek Painter's Guide from Mount Athos* the scene of Samson and the Lion is alone mentioned, that of David being omitted. Perhaps this may be accounted for by the fact that the former comes first in an historical series, and being so like the other, and involving the same symbolism, its repetition with David for the hero instead of Samson was unnecessary, and would only lead to confusion. The conventional method of representing the Killing of the Lion is the same in both cases, although the Scriptural account is somewhat different. In the Book of Judges (xiv, 6) we read of Samson, that he " rent the lion as he would have rent a kid"; but David says, when the lion rose against him (1 Samuel xvii, 35), " I caught him by his beard and smote him and slew him." The bear mentioned in the latter account is generally omitted.

Scenes from the Life of David do not occur in early Christian art in the Catacombs, with the solitary exception of David holding a sling, of which there is only one example, nor are they to be seen on the sculptured sarcophagi. In later times, when the ritual of the Church became more developed, the

Fig. 64.—David and the Lion on sculptured slab at St. Andrews.

Psalter was one of the regular service-books, and the illuminations of the MSS. consisted either of scenes from the Life of David, pictures illustrative of the words of the Psalmist, or series of the Life of Christ. Many of the early Psalters were divided into three parts, having an illuminated initial page, with a full-page miniature opposite, at the beginning of the 1st, the 51st, and the 101st Psalm, and it is here that we generally find the exploits of David illustrated. In the thirteenth century the divisions were liturgical, and the Psalms with initial letters referring to the opening words are those with which the services

commenced on each day of the week according to the Roman
and Salisbury uses.[1] There are other Psalters which are illustrated throughout, either with marginal drawings[2] or pictures in
the text, giving a literal interpretation of the words of the
Psalms.[3]

Several Irish[4] and Anglo-Saxon[5] Psalters are in existence, containing scenes from the Life of David, of which the following

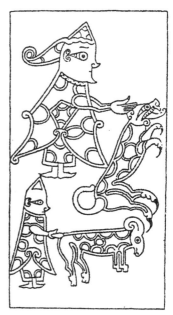

Fig. 66.—David and Goliath, and David and the Lion, from Irish Psalter of
St. John's College, Cambridge.

are the most common :—David playing the harp with his four
assistants, which usually forms the frontispiece to the volume ;

[1] W. de Gray Birch, *Early Drawings and Illuminations in the British
Museum,* p. 252—Sun., Ps. 1 ; Mon.. Ps. 26 ; Tues., Ps. 38 ; Wed., Ps. 52 ;
Thurs., Ps. 68 ; Fri., Ps. 97 ; Sat., Ps. 101 ; Sun., Ps. 109.

[2] Greek Psalter, A.D. 1066, Brit. Mus. (Add. MS. 19,352).

[3] Utrecht Psalter. (See W. de G. Birch.)

[4] Brit. Mus., Vit. F. xi ; St. John's Coll., Cambridge.

[5] Brit. Mus., Vesp. A. i ; Tib. C. vi ; Boulogne Public Lib. ; Cambridge Univ. Lib. ; Durham Cath. Lib., Cassiodorus Commentary. (See
Westwood's *Miniatures* and *Palæographia.*)

slaying the lion; attacking Goliath with sling; cuttting off
Goliath's head with sword; carrying Goliath's head to Saul;
and sometimes the anointing by Samuel. Out of these, two occur
very frequently on Celtic sculptured stones,—David playing on
the harp, which subject has been discussed in the last lecture,
and David slaying the Lion, which is to be seen on four of the
Irish crosses[1] and on two stones in Scotland.[2] On one of the
panels of the shaft of the Great Cross at Monasterboice is what
may possibly be a representation of the Anointing of David by
Samuel. The Celtic sculptors naturally reproduced upon the
crosses those scenes which were constantly before their eyes in
the illuminations of the MSS., but David and the Lion seems
to have been specially chosen in preference to the others, because
it belongs to that class which, like Daniel in the Lion's Den,
Noah in the Ark, and the other cycle of scenes found in the
paintings of the Catacombs, set forth God's power to save the
faithful from spiritual danger. In the *Biblia Pauperum*[3] a
resemblance is traced between the mouth of hell, which in
mediæval art is always symbolised by the open mouth of
a monster, and the jaws of the lion rent by Samson. Thus the
type and antitype are placed side by side,—Christ delivering
Adam from Limbus in the centre; on the right Samson and
the Lion; and on the left David and Goliath. The same idea
is carried out in the thirteenth century windows of Chartres
Cathedral.[4]

The triumph of man in his contest with wild beasts has
always been a favourite subject in pagan as well as Christian
art, and the representations of Samson and David slaying the
lion bear a marked resemblance to Gistubar on Assyrian sculptures,[5] and Hercules and the Lion in Roman mythology. In a
Byzantine MS. of the ninth century, in the Imperial Library at
Paris,[6] there is a miniature of David with a club killing the lion,
which is devouring one of the sheep, and behind him is a personi-

---

[1] Monasterboice, Kells (two crosses), Durrow. (See O'Neill, pls. 19, 29,
34.)

[2] St. Andrew's, Drainie. (See *Stuart*, vol. i, pls. 61 and 130.)

[3] J. Ph. Berjeau's reprint.

[4] Didron, *Monographie de la Cathédrale de Chartres.*

[5] *Journ. Brit. Archæol. Assoc.*, vol. xli, p. 398.

[6] Mrs. Jameson's *Life of Our Lord*, vol. i, p. 204.

fication of force with a nimbus round the head, and the inscription 'Ισχύς above. The bear is already dead, and a harp lies on the ground.

The Sacrifice of Isaac.

Upon the second panel from the bottom of the shaft of the Great Cross at Monasterboice is a sculpture of the Sacrifice of Isaac. This subject has always been a favourite one throughout the whole range of Christian art, and as the description given in Genesis (xxii, 1-14) is generally strictly adhered to, the traditional features of the scene do not vary to any great extent. From the time of St. Paul (Heb. xi, 17) onwards the Sacrifice of Isaac was universally acknowledged as a symbol of faith, and as foreshadowing the greater sacrifice of Christ upon the cross. St. Gregory of Nyssa, who was born about A.D. 331, alludes to the frequency of such representations, and tells us that he often could not refrain from tears, " beholding Isaac, with his hands bound behind his back, and Abraham with one hand grasping the hair of his son, while looking down on him with sorrow, and in the other hand holding the weapon raised to strike."[1] The subject occurs frequently on the paintings in the Catacombs,[2] and on about eleven out of fifty sarcophagi[3] in the Lateran Museum at Rome. The earliest dated example is probably on the sarcophagus of Junius Bassus (A.D. 359),[4] to which we have had to refer so often as one of the most important landmarks in the history of Christian art. Here Abraham, clad in long flowing garments, stands in the centre with one hand upraised, holding a sword ready to strike, and the other placed upon the head of Isaac, who kneels at his feet on the right, with his hands tied behind his back. The hand of the angel of God is shown above on the left, holding back the sword. In front of Isaac is the altar with fire burning upon it, and on the other side of Abraham is the ram (or, as it is here shown, a lamb) caught in a thicket (Gen. xxii, 13). The reason for this deviation from historical accuracy, in replacing the ram by a lamb, is that the

---

[1] Conc. Nic., ii, Act 4 ; quoted in Mrs. Jameson's Hist. of Our Lord, vol. i, p. 133.

[2] Garrucci, Storia del Arte Cristiana, vol. ii, pls. 24, 48, 69, 71, 77.

[3] Northcote and Brownlow's Roma Sotterranea, vol. ii, p. 262.

[4] Appell's Monuments of Early Christian Art, p. 9.

early commentators saw in the ram a type of Christ crucified or crowned with thorns, and therefore the Agnus Dei was preferred to the ram. A third human figure is introduced standing by the side of Abraham, which is probably one of the two young men he took with him (Gen. xxii, 3).

The early representations do not always follow the exact words of Scripture, in showing Isaac "laid on the altar, upon the wood" (Gen. xxii, 9), but place him sometimes kneeling beside the altar, with his hands tied behind him. Isaac is in many cases bound as well as blindfolded. The moment immediately preceding the sacrifice where " Abraham took the wood of the burnt-offering and laid it upon Isaac his son; and he took the fire in his hand and a knife; and they both of them went together" (Gen. xxii, 6), is chosen by the artist in some instances, especially in the thirteenth century, and there are also representations of Abraham after the sacrifice in an attitude of prayer, with Isaac standing upright on one side near the altar, and the ram on the other.[1] In the thirteenth century windows of Bourges Cathedral,[2] and in the *Biblia Pauperum*,[3] we see Isaac carrying two sticks over his shoulders, placed so as to form a cross, side by side with Christ carrying His cross, and a fanciful resemblance was traced between the wood carried by Isaac and the two sticks gathered by the widow of Zarephath (1 Kings xvii, 12). There is a passage in Bede's *Lives of the Holy Abbots*[4] bearing on the subject, which is of the highest interest as throwing light on early Christian symbolism in this country. It is as follows:

" Now when Benedict (Biscop) had made this man (Easterwine) Abbot of St. Peter's (Monkwearmouth), and Ceolfrid Abbot of St. Paul's (Jarrow), he not long after made his fifth voyage[5] from Britain to Rome, and returned, as usual, with an immense number of proper ecclesiastical relics. There were many sacred books and pictures of the saints, as numerous as before. He also brought with him pictures of our Lord's history, which he hung round

---

[1] God blessing Abraham after the Sacrifice occurs on a twelfth century ivory plaque at Salerno Cathedral. (Westwood, *Catal.*, p. 94.)

[2] Miss Twining's *Symbols and Emblems*, pl. 20.

[3] Facsimile, by J. P. Berjeau.

[4] J. A. Giles's translation, vol. iv, p. 375.

[5] About A.D. 685.

the Chapel of Our Lady in the larger monastery ; and others to adorn St. Paul's Church and Monastery, ably describing the connection of the Old and the New Testament,—as, for instance, Isaac bearing the wood for his sacrifice, and Christ carrying the cross on which He was about to suffer, were placed side by side. Again, the serpent raised up by Moses in the desert was illustrated by the Son of Man upon the cross. Among other things, he brought two cloaks, all of silk and of incomparable workmanship, for which he received an estate of three hides on the south bank of the River Wear, near its mouth, from King Alfrid."

On the station-cross at Mayence,[1] of the twelfth century, are a most important series of Old and New Testament types, similar to those described by Bede, and all inscribed. The central panel on the back is occupied by the Sacrifice of Isaac inscribed with the first part of a hexameter verse,—" Cui patriarcha suum", which is finished round the corresponding medallion on the front enclosing the Agnus Dei,—" Pater offert in cruce natum."

- I cannot find any representations of the Sacrifice of Isaac in Irish MSS., and only two or three in Saxon ones, at the beginning of the *Psycomachia* of Prudentius,[2] and in Ælfric's *Heptateuch*,[3] where the subject is treated historically in several scenes.

Besides the Great Cross at Monasterboice there are seven others[4] where this subject occurs. The scene is treated in a most conventional way, the chief peculiarity being the attitude. Isaac bends over the altar like a man on a block preparing to be beheaded. Above the bent body of Isaac is the ram ; and Abraham, standing erect with a sword in his hand, occupies the rest of the picture. On the cross at Moone Abbey, Abraham is seated on a high-backed chair. On the Great Cross at Monasterboice, on the two crosses at Kells, and on the one at Arboe, Isaac is engaged chopping the wood for the sacrifice on

---

[1] St. J. Tyrwhitt's *Art Teaching of the Primitive Church*, p. 251.

[2] Brit. Mus., eleventh century (Add. MS. 24,199, and Tit. D. xvi).

[3] Brit. Mus., eleventh century (Claud. B. iv).

[4] Ullard, Moone Abbey, Arboe, Castle Dermot (two crosses), and Kells (two crosses). (See *O'Neill*, pls. 9, 18, 23, 28, 31.)

the altar; and there is at Monasterboice and Arboe an additional
figure close to the ram, which may be intended for the angel, or
perhaps Abraham's servant. There is, however, no indication
of the Dextera Dei, or Hand symbol, which is seen in most early
representations.

In Norman sculpture the Sacrifice of Isaac is a very rare
subject, and I only know of one example,[1] on the tympanum
of a doorway at Rochester Cathedral. It is almost entirely
destroyed by exposure to the weather, but the Hand symbol and
the words ARIES PER CORNVA, which formed part of an inscription running round the whole, can still be clearly distinguished.

Fig. 66.—Sacrifice of Isaac—(1) on arm of Cross of SS. Patrick and Columba at Kells,
and (2) on shaft of Great Cross at Monasterboice.

An eighteenth century tombstone in Logierait churchyard in
Perthshire presents a very remarkable instance of the survival,
or perhaps revival, of ancient symbolism. Here, side by side
with the skull and cross-bones, the hour-glass, the spade, and the
coffin, which enabled a gloomy generation to remind the living
of the horrors of death, we have a representation of the Sacrifice of Isaac, recalling the beautiful symbolism of the early
Christians, who looked upon death as the gate of eternal life.
Abraham wears the dress of the eighteenth century, and holds
a knife in his hand, as described in our version of the Bible,
not a sword, as is commonly seen in early examples. Isaac in

[1] In France it occurs on the capital of a column at St. Benoit sur
Loire ; De Caumont's *Abécédaire d'Archéologie*, p. 213.

a kilt is lying on the altar, with his hands tied and his legs dangling over the side. Abraham has one hand placed on the head of Isaac, whilst the other is being held back by a very quaint figure of an angel. Below is the ram, caught in the bush, and an open book has the words, "Abraham offering up Isaac is stayed by an Angel" (Gen. xxii). The date is 1774.

Fig. 67.—Sacrifice of Isaac, on eighteenth century tombstone at Logierait.

There seems to have been a revival[1] of ancient symbolism in Puritan times, but whether the representations of Scripture scenes belonging to the seventeenth and eighteenth centuries were copied from old woodcuts, or designed afresh from the texts in the Bible, it is difficult to say. The Temptation of

[1] Or perhaps a survival, in Germany, which influenced this country by articles manufactured there and exported.

Adam and Eve[1] and the Sacrifice of Isaac[2] were placed on tombstones even within the present century; and the same scenes are to be found on carved woodwork used in the decoration of houses in the sixteenth century, there being a very curious example over the chimney-piece of a farm-house at Swayfield in Lincolnshire,[3] where Abraham is dressed in the trunk hose of the period. A panel of about the same date, with the Sacrifice of Isaac on it, found in London, is engraved in the *Journal of the British Archæological Association.*[4] Other survivals of the same class are to be found on a carved wooden peg tankard of the fifteenth century in the **Ashmolean Museum** at Oxford,[5] with Jacob's Dream, the Sacrifice of Isaac, and King David; two fire-dogs in the South Kensington Museum, dated 1549, with Adam and Eve, Samson and the Lion, Samson carrying away the Gates of Gaza, David playing the Harp, and the Crucifixion; and on seventeenth century Scandinavian powder-horns, with Adam and Eve, Samson, David, etc., of which there are several specimens in the Edinburgh Museum of Antiquities.

The Three Children in the Furnace.

Upon the top panel of the shaft of the Great Cross at Monasterboice, on the same side as Christ in Glory, is a sculpture which seems to be intended for the Three Children in the Fiery Furnace. Under a kind of arch with flames issuing from it, which represents the door of the furnace, are three little kneeling figures, and on each side is a man with a lump of fuel on a two-pronged fork. A similar representation occurs on two other crosses in Ireland,[6] but I do not remember any instances on sculptured stones in other parts of Great Britain, or in the Irish or Saxon MSS. of the same period. This subject is found frequently in the paintings in the Catacombs, but on the sculptured sarcophagi it is less common, being only seen on four out of fifty in the Lateran Museum, examined by Dean Burgon.

[1] St. John Leonard, Gloucestershire, 1834.

[2] Horsham, Sussex, 1835.

[3] Ashby-de-la-Zouche, *Anastatic Drawing Soc.*, 1863, pl. 53.

[4] Vol. xxxii, p. 242.

[5] Illustrated in Shaw's *Specimens of Ancient Furniture.*

[6] Kells and Arboe. *(O'Neill*, pls. 28, 31.)

We have the testimony of St. Cyprian[1] that the early Christians were encouraged to profess their faith without fear of death by martyrdom, believing that they would be delivered, as were the Three Children, who openly acknowledged their belief in the true God regardless of consequences. St. Irenæus and St. Turtullian saw in the Three Children a type of the Resurrec-

Fig. 68.—The Three Children in the Fiery Furnace, etc., on the shaft of the Cross of SS. Patrick and Columba at Kells.

tion and St. Cyril of Alexandria compares the furnace to the Church, where men may in concert with angels continually do homage to the Saviour.[2] In the hymns of St. Ephrem[3] the

[1] Epist. lxi, ed. Baluz ; quoted by Martigny, and Northcote and Brownlow.

[2] Martigny's *Dict.*, art. "Hébreux", p. 340.

[3] Hymn 43 ; quoted by Northcote and Brownlow, *Roma Sotterranea*, vol. ii, p. 113.

stories of Daniel in the Lion's Den, the Three Children, and
Jonah, are associated together as having one meaning. " The
body," it is said, " has triumphed over the lion's den, over the
fiery furnace, over the monstrous fish, which was obliged to
surrender him whom it had swallowed."

The word children does not, of course, refer to the age of the
Israelites in question, but means that they were descendants or
children of Judah, as mentioned in the first chapter of Daniel.
We learn from the Bible that their names were originally
Hananiah, Misael, and Azariah, which were afterwards changed
by the prince of the Eunuchs to Shadrach, Mesech, and Abed-
nego (Dan. i, 7).

The connection between the Three Children and the Magi
may be partly due to the former being described as being skilful
in all wisdom (Dan. i, 4), and the Magi being called wise men.
The Three Children are also mentioned as being of royal descent
(Dan. i, 3). The scene of the Three Children refusing to
worship the image, which is of much rarer occurrence than the
Three Children in the Furnace, is the one which is placed side
by side with the Adoration of the Magi on some of the sarcophagi and the later paintings in the Catacombs.[1] The early
conventional representation of the Three Children in the Fiery
Furnace consists of three figures, " in their coats, their hosen,
and their hats, and their other garments" (Dan. iii, 21), standing
with their hands upraised in the ancient attitude of prayer on
the top of a furnace, having flames issuing from its three doors.
The headgear consists of Phrygian caps, similar to those worn
by the Magi. The fourth figure, "like the Son of God'
(Dan. iii, 25), is hardly ever seen. The *Greek Painter's Guide
from Mount Athos* gives the following description : " A furnace
within, the three children fully dressed, the hands and face
lifted to heaven ; the Archangel Michael in the midst of them ;
the soldiers are devoured by the flames. Hard by is erected the
King's image."

The Three Children in the Furnace is not a subject which
occurs in Norman sculpture, and is rare in later mediæval art,

---

[1] *Northcote and Brownlow*, vol. ii, p. 114 ; Martigny's *Dict.*, article
" Hébreux", p. 338.

[2] Didron, *Guide de la Peinture*, p. 118.

although it sometimes is seen as a type of the Last Judgment, in allusion to being saved by Christ from fire. In the *Biblia Pauperum* the scene is associated with the Transfiguration, and Abraham and the Three Angels.

Soldiers guarding the Sepulchre.

Before leaving the Great Cross at Monasterboice a subject must be noticed which occupies the bottom panel of the shaft on the opposite side to those just described. The sculpture, which is a good deal defaced, seems to show two soldiers with helmets and spears bending over a tomb, and a cross in the centre. Similar representations occur on two other Irish crosses, at Kells and Clonmacnois, and it is supposed to be intended for the Soldiers watching the Sepulchre of Christ (Matt. xxvii, 66). If this is the case, the three small crosses on the tomb, which appear in the bottom panel of the cross of King Fland at Clonmacnois, may be the seals on the stone. In the *Greek Painter's Guide from Mount Athos*[1] four seals are specified. The scene belongs to the series of the Passion, and comes between the Entombment and the Descent into Limbus.

MOONE ABBEY CROSS.

Having exhaustively examined the symbolism of the crosses at Monasterboice, we will now turn to some of the other monuments of the same class in Ireland which present new subjects.

In the churchyard of Moone Abbey, which lies eight miles east of Athy, in the county of Kildare, is a very fine granite cross in admirable preservation. It is 12 ft. 9 ins. high, and measures 4 ft. across the arms. The shape of the head is the same as that of the other Irish crosses, but the lower part is somewhat different, there being only a short shaft, then an intermediate piece with sloping sides, and lastly, the base with sides which are more nearly perpendicular. On one face of the head of the cross is the figure of the Saviour crucified, with His arms extended, and a sort of fish or dolphin above the head. The rest of the sculpture on the upper part of the cross consists of little panels, enclosing single figures of men and animals and

---

[1] Didron, *Guide de la Peinture*, p. 199.

geometrical ornament. The middle part of the cross between the shaft and the base has a panel of sculpture on each of the four sides: (1) the Crucifixion; (2) the Temptation of Adam and Eve; (3) two figures seated on thrones facing each other, and with a circular disc between them; (4) three little figures under an arch, and an angel with four wings above.

Fig. 69.—Middle part of Moone Abbey Cross.

The base has on the front a single panel, enclosing twelve figures arranged in three rows, perhaps intended for the Apostles; on the back two panels—(1) the Sacrifice of Isaac; (2) Daniel in the Lions' Den; on one side two panels—(1) the Flight into Egypt; (2) a pair of fishes facing each other, with five circular objects below, and a long fish on each side. Perhaps these are symbolical of the miracle of the multiplication of the loaves and fishes; on the other side two panels—(1) Man between two figures with human bodies and beasts' heads; (2) four serpents and two beasts interlaced.

Daniel in the Lions' Den.

Most of these subjects have been already discussed, but there are others which we have not met with before.   Daniel in the Lions' Den has been described by Dr. J. Anderson in a previous course of Rhind Lectures,[1] and also in a very interesting paper read by him before the Society of Antiquaries of Scotland.[2]

Fig 70.—Daniel in the Lions' Den, etc., on the base of the Moone Abbey Cross.

The early Christians, following the example of Darius (Dan. vi, 26-27), looked upon the delivery of Daniel from the power of the lions as a proof that God will stand by those who believe on Him, and rescue them from the dominion of evil.   By St. Irenæus and Tertullian Daniel in the Lions' Den was used as a symbol of the Resurrection.[3]

In the prayers for the dead in the early liturgies, and on an inscribed glass plate of the fifth century found at Podgoritza in Albania, the same meaning is attached to the delivery of Daniel from the Den of Lions, the Three Children from the Fiery

[1] *Scotland in Early Christian Times*, 2nd Series, pp. 144 to 150.

[2] Vol. xi, p. 388.

[3] Northcote and Brownlow's *Roma Sotterranea*, vol. ii, p. 113.

Furnace, Susanna from a false accusation, and Jonah from the
Whale's Belly.[1] Daniel in the Lions' Den is found frequently
on paintings in the Catacombs at Rome, the most ancient example
being perhaps of the second or third century, in the cemetery of
Domitilla.[2] He is represented as a nude figure, with his two
hands upraised in the ancient attitude of prayer, and with a lion
on each side looking towards him. On the sarcophagus of
Junius Bassus the subject is similarly treated, but the figure of
a man on each side is added, supposed by Martigny to be the
Persian satraps who condemned the Prophet. On some of the
sarcophagi Abacuc is seen carried by the hair of the head to
Babylon,[3] or bringing food to Daniel,[4] as described in the
Apocrypha. Daniel feeding the Dragon with balls of pitch[5]
occurs in a few cases. On the later sarcophagi the Prophet is
clothed, and wears a Phrygian cap, and sometimes the number
of the lions is increased from two to four. The meaning of this
subject is proved beyond possibility of doubt by the numerous
inscribed examples found engraved on belt-clasps from Bur-
gundian graves.[6] The only instance I have seen in a MS. of
Daniel in the Lions' Den treated after the ancient conventional
fashion, is in the Spanish Apocalypse of the twelfth century in
the British Museum.[7]

It will be noticed that on the Moone Abbey cross the number
of lions given in the Vulgate is adhered to, namely, seven, there
being three on the right and four on the left. This is the number
also specified in the *Greek Painter's Guide from Mount Athos.*
As a general rule, however, symmetry is preferred to historical
accuracy, two and four being the most common number of lions.

[1] *Scotland in Early Christian Times*, 2nd Series, p. 152.

[2] *Northcote and Brownlow*, vol. ii, p. 123.

[3] Appell's *Monuments of Early Christian Art*, p. 31 ; Sarcophagus in
Brescia Museum ; *Proc. Soc. Ant. Scot.*, vol. xi, p. 390—Bucket from
Miannay ; Tympanum of doorway of Chapel of St. Gabriel, near
Tarascon in France. H. Revoil, *Architecture Romane du Midi de la
France*, vol. i, p. 17.

[4] *Appell*, p. 16—St. Paul's extra Muros, Rome.

[5] Martigny's *Dict.*, art. " Daniel", p. 236.

[6] Found chiefly in Savoy, and the Jura, Switzerland. (Le Blant,
Inscr. Chrét. de la Gaule ; Troyon, in *Zürich Ant. Soc.*, vol. ii.)

[7] Add. MS. No. 11,695.

Daniel in the Lions' Den occurs 'very frequently on Celtic sculptured stonework, and is to be found on seven crosses in Ireland and . six in Scotland.   After the twelfth century the subject becomes rare ; but there is a very remarkable piece of Norman sculpture on the west front of Lincoln Cathedral, representing Daniel draped and seated, holding a book, with five lions round him, two above facing outwards, and three below, looking towards the prophet.   The only scene from the Life of Daniel in the *Biblia Pauperum* is his accusal by the Babylonians.

On an ivory plaque of the tenth century, in the collection of M. Uzielli, of which there is a cast in the South Kensington Museum (Westwood's *Catal.*, No. 274), the scene of Daniel in

Fig. 71.—Daniel in the Lions' Den, on Cross at Meigle, in Perthshire.

the Lions' Den includes King Darius and Habakkuk, held up by the hair of the head by an angel.

The Flight into Egypt.

The Flight into Egypt, which is seen on the base of the Moone Abbey cross, belongs not to the symbolical representations found in the paintings in the Catacombs and on the sculptured sarcophagi, but to the regular series of the Life of Christ, which first make their appearance in Christian art in about the tenth or eleventh century, and become exceedingly common in the thirteenth and fourteenth centuries.   The sculpture shows the Virgin and Child seated upon an ass, which is being led by Joseph.   In the Gospel of St. Matthew, the only one of the four Evangelists who describes the Flight into

Egypt, no particulars are given beyond that Joseph, being warned by an angel in a dream, " arose, betook the young child and his mother by night, and departed into Egypt" (Matt. ii, 14). The method of travelling adopted in art, and consistently adhered to, was probably that in vogue at the time when the scene was first introduced. The *Greek Painter's Guide* describes Joseph as walking behind the ass[1] on which the Virgin is seated, and also introduces an attendant leading another ass laden with a basket of rushes. Sometimes an angel is directing them on

Fig. 72.—The Flight into Egypt, etc., on the base of the Moone Abbey Cross.

their journey, or the Hand of God is seen issuing from a cloud to express the same thing. In the apocryphal Gospel of the Infancy of Jesus Christ[2] (iv, 6-13), it is related that as soon as our Lord entered Egypt, the idol which the inhabitants of that country worshipped, on being questioned, told the people that the unknown God, who is truly God, had come amongst them, and having thus spoken, the idol fell down. The same story is told in the

[1] The Feast of the Ass was anciently celebrated at Beauvais on the 14th of January, to commemorate the Flight into Egypt (see Hone's *Mysteries*, p. 161). The cross on the back of the ass is traditionally believed to have been placed there by God, in consequence of his having been ridden upon by Christ when entering Jerusalem.

[2] Hone's edition.

Golden Legend,[1] which calls the name of the city of Egypt Hermopolis, and also mentions a tree, which bowed down in adoration of the Saviour as He passed by. The fall of the idol is referred to in the *Greek Painter's Guide*, and it is illustrated in the *Biblia Pauperum* side by side with the Adoration of the Golden Calf and Dagon falling before the Ark. The story evidently originates in the text in St. Matthew's Gospel (ii, 15), quoting the prophecy of Hosea (xi, 1), "and called my son out of Egypt", the following verse being, "As they called them so they went from them; they sacrificed unto Baalim, and burned incense to graven images." The rest is founded on the prophecies of Isaiah (xix, 3, 19-22).

Dr. J. Anderson recognises the Fall of the Idols on the arm of the cross in the Street of Kells.

I do not know of any miniature of the Flight into Egypt in the Irish or Celtic MSS., but the subject occurs in MSS.,[2] sculptured details of churches,[3] and on ivories,[4] in the eleventh and twelfth centuries. The description of the Return from Egypt in the Gospel corresponds so nearly with that of the Flight, that, except in the *Biblia Pauperum* and in the diffuse series of the Life of Christ in later mediæval art, it was not considered necessary to represent both.

Enthroned Figures.

One of the panels of the middle portion of the Moone Abbey cross has upon it a pair of enthroned figures facing each other, and holding a circular disc between them. No satisfactory explanation of the meaning of this representation can be given, but several other similar ones may be seen on pre-Norman

---

[1] Didron, *Guide de la Peinture*, p. 160.

[2] Brit. Mus. (Nero C. iv).

[3] Cap of column, St. Benoit sur Loire, France (De Caumont's *Abécédaire d'Archéologie*, p. 257); St. Maire a Toscanella, Italy (Gailhabaud's *Architecture*, vol. ii, Part I); Pulpit at S. Michele, Groppoli (*Builder*, Dec. 10th, 1881).

[4] Plaques of shrine, Salerno Cath., Italy; Carlovingian Casket in the Louvre. (Westwood's *Catalogue of the Fictile Ivories in the South Kensington Museum*, pp. 93 and 231.)

sculptured stones in Scotland,[1] the Isle of Man,[2] and England,[3] in many cases associated with 'the elephant, double disc, crescent and V-shaped rod and other symbols, one of the best examples being at Dunfallandy in Perthshire.

Fig. 73.—Pair of enthroned figures holding disc, on Cross at St. Vigeans.

Thrones are continually mentioned throughout the Bible, especially the throne of David, of Christ, and of God. Perhaps the most important text bearing on the subject is in the Revela-

tions (iii, 21), "To him that overcometh will I grant to sit with
me in my throne, even as I also overcame, and am set down
with my Father in his throne." It is possible that the enthroned figures on the sculptured stones may be intended for

Fig. 74.—Circular Disc or Loaf held in Bird's Mouth, on the Cross at Nigg.

ecclesiastical dignitaries or kings, but they do not hold croziers
or wear crowns. Sometimes there is only a single figure on a
throne, and sometimes a pair of figures seated side by side on

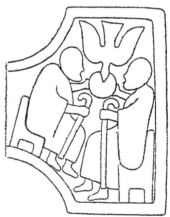

Fig. 75.—Bird holding circular Disc, with Ecclesiastics on each side—(1) on Cross in Street
of Kells, and (2) on Cross of SS. Patrick and Columba at Kells.

one throne. The circular disc (generally held in the mouth of
a bird) between two ecclesiastics occurs on crosses at Nigg,
Ross-shire; Kirriemuir and St. Vigeans, Forfarshire; Kells,
co. Meath; Monasterboice, co. Louth; and Castledermot, co.
Kildare. It may be that this subject is intended for St. Paul

and St. Anthony breaking bread in the desert, as represented on the inscribed cross at Ruthwell in Dumfriesshire.

Fig. 76.—Miracle of the Loaves and Fishes, on bases of two Crosses at Castledermot, co. Kildare.

Miracle of the Loaves and Fishes.

The sculpture on the base of the Moone Abbey cross, of two fishes and five circular discs, which are probably symbolical of

Q

the miracle of the Multiplication of the Loaves and Fishes, is almost unique as far as the art of this country is concerned,[1] the only other instances being on the bases of the two crosses at Castledermot, co. Kildare, apparently executed by the same artist ; and on the top panel of the cross in the town of Kells. In the paintings in the Catacombs there are several representations of loaves and fishes,[2] which are supposed to have reference either to the feeding of five thousand with five loaves and two fishes (Matt. xiv, 17), or feeding four thousand with seven loaves and a few little fishes (Matt. xv, 34), or to our Lord's feast with His disciples, described in the last chapter of St. John (xxi, 13).

St. Augustine considered that the last of these was typical of the Sacrament of the Lord's Supper (Piscis assus, Christus passus). A most curious monument, having on it two fishes and seven loaves marked with a cross, was found at Modena, inscribed with the name SYNTROPHION.[3] The fishes are facing each other and the loaves in a straight row between them. The symbolism of the Moone Abbey cross is of the same abstract nature, but it refers to the first of the two miracles of the Multiplication of the Loaves and Fishes, instead of the second, and the loaves are arranged not in a row, but like the spots on a die. On the crosses at Castledermot the figures of Christ holding one of the loaves, and the disciples, are introduced. On the cross in the town of Kells, our Lord is seated, having five loaves in His right hand and two crossed fishes in His left.

CROSSES AT KELLS.

Next to Clonmacnois and Monasterboice, Kells, in the county of Meath, must have been one of the most important schools of early art in Ireland, as is clearly proved by the architectural remains and sculptured crosses still existing there, and the illuminated MSS. and metalwork which it has produced. Kells was the site of the royal dun or fort of Diarmait Mac Cerbhaill, and St. Columba is supposed to have founded a church here in

---

[1] A curious example of this subject occurs on an ivory plaque of the eleventh century at Salerno Cathedral. (S. K. Mus. Cast, 1874, 103.)

[2] Northcote and Brownlow's Roma Sotterranea, vol. ii, p. 66.

[3] Martigny's Dict., art. " Poisson ", p. 658.

the sixth century; but the place does not seem to have risen into eminence until A.D. 804, when, on account of the dangers to which the community at Iona was exposed, an asylum was found for them at Kells, which henceforth became the chief seat of the Columbian monks in Ireland.[1] The works of art in metal connected with this place are the crozier now in the British Museum,[2] made for Maelfinnen, Bishop of Kells, who died A.D. 968, and the Cathac, or shrine of Columba's Psalter,[3] in the Museum of the Royal Irish Academy at Dublin, made by Sitric Mac Aeda, artificer, of Kells, for Cathbar O'Donnell, who died A.D. 1106.

The finest Celtic MS. ever executed is known as the *Book of Kells*, and is now preserved in the Library of Trinity College, Dublin. The volume has been associated with Kells since the year A.D. 1006, when its shrine is recorded, in the *Annals of the Four Masters*, to have been stolen in the night, and it contains grants of land to the Abbey of Kells, by Melaghlin, King of Meath, A.D. 1152. It remained amongst the chief treasures of the monastery until the time of Archbishop Ussher (A.D. 1621-1624), when it was transferred, with the rest of his library, to Trinity College, Dublin.[4]

The remains still existing at Kells consist of a round tower 90 feet high, a stone-roofed church called "St. Columkille's House", and three elaborately sculptured crosses, similar to those at Monasterboice and other places in Ireland; one stands in the churchyard near the round tower, and bears an inscription in minuscules on its base—

"PATRICII ET COLUMBE (CRUX)"

("The cross of SS. Patrick and Columba"); the shaft of the second has been erected on the old base, but its head lies in a mutilated condition in the churchyard; and the third, although much damaged, still stands in a street near the market-place of the town of Kells.

The cross of SS. Patrick and Columba in the churchyard is 11 ft. high, including the base, which is 1 ft. 9 ins. high, and

---

[1] Petrie's *Irish Inscriptions*, vol. ii, p. 63.

[2] *Ibid.*, p. 116.   [3] *Ibid.*, p. 91.

[4] Westwood's *Miniatures*, p. 25.

measures 3 ft. 2 ins. across the arms. On the front, in the
centre of the cross, is Christ in Glory, holding the cross and
sceptre, with a beast on each side ; above, within a circular
medallion, held up by two arms, the Agnus Dei ; and below, on
the shaft, is the Crucifixion (see figs. 34 and 46). On the back
we have on the top arm David playing the harp, and another
figure with two crossed fish below, perhaps intended to
symbolise the miracle of the Loaves and Fishes, as on the
cross in the town of Kells ; on the right arm, two ecclesiastics
seated on thrones and holding croziers, with a bird holding

Fig. 77.—Two sides of the base of the Cross of SS. Patrick and Columba at Kells.

a circular disc between them[1] ; on the left arm, the Sacrifice
of Isaac, much defaced, and on the shaft Daniel in the Lions'
Den ; the Three Children in the Fiery Furnace ; and the Temptation and Expulsion of Adam and Eve (see fig. 68). On the sides
are two ecclesiastics with books, seated side by side ; David
and the Bear ; a bull and another animal ; and David and the
Lion. All these subjects have been already described except
the Agnus Dei. A similar representation occurs on the cross
at Durrow, King's County, but I do not know of any other

[1] This subject also occurs on the two crosses at Castledermot, co. Kildare ; at Kells, and at Nigg in Ross-shire.

instance of it on Celtic sculptured stones, or in the Irish MSS. of the period.[1]

Two sides of the socket-stones of the cross are covered with interlaced ornament, and the remaining two have figure-sculpture, consisting of a chariot containing two persons and drawn by a horse, with an animal and two men on horseback in front; a stag, a bird, and other animals. There are several other crosses in Ireland which have carved socket-stones,[2] and the scenes represented are not so obviously Scriptural as those on the shafts and heads, and in this respect, as well as in other particulars, they have more in common with the crosses of the East of

Fig. 78.—One side of the base of the Cross of Muiredach at Monasterboice.

Scotland than anything to be found elsewhere. For instance, the chariots on the bases of the crosses at Kells and Kilklispeen in Ireland, correspond with the figures on one of the slabs at Meigle in Perthshire,[3] now destroyed, but of which an engraving has been preserved. The hunting scenes, the warriors, the centaurs, birds, beasts, and the ecclesiastics with peaked hoods behind their heads on the same crosses, all have their counterparts on the Scotch stones. The centaurs and animals will be referred to in a future lecture on the mediæval bestiaries.

Chariots.—With regard to the chariots, we must suppose that

[1] The Agnus Dei occurs in a Saxon MS. of the eleventh century in the British Museum (Tib. C. vi).

[2] Kilklispeen, Monasterboice, Kells (2), Castledermot (2), Clonmacnois.

[3] Stuart's *Sculptured Stones*, vol. i, pl. 76.

they represent the usual method of locomotion of the period, or else that they are intended for the chariots forming a feature in some-Scripture scene. In the Old Testament chariots are very frequently mentioned, generally as being used in warfare, but more rarely for ordinary means of getting from one place to another. Sometimes, also, chariots are made use of in a figurative sense. In the New Testament the word chariot only occurs once, in the description of the meeting of St. Philip and the Eunuch (Acts viii, 29). Out of all these passages, however, only two are illustrated in Christian art, namely, the Destruction of Pharaoh's Hosts in the Red Sea, and the Ascent of Elijah, both of which subjects are chosen on account of their special symbolical bearing on the doctrines of Christianity. The Passage of the Red Sea is used as a type of Baptism, and the Pursuit of Pharaoh was supposed to signify the attempts of the enemies of the soul to place obstacles in its path.

The Translation of Elijah was typical of the Ascension of Christ, and his mantle falling on Elisha foreshadowed the spirit and office of our Lord descending upon the Apostles after His passing out of this world to the Father. The Destruction of Pharaoh's Host, as seen on the sculptured sarcophagi, includes a great number of figures; on the centre, chariots, men, and horses in great confusion perishing in the Red Sea; on one bank, Pharaoh, with other horses and chariots, advancing in pursuit, and on the other Moses and the Israelites, who have passed safely over, leading their children by the hands.[1] The chief features in the Ascent of Elijah as represented on sculptured sarcophagi, ivories, and in Byzantine MSS., are Elijah driving a chariot with four horses, and his mantle falling from him into the hands of Elisha, who stands behind. Below is a personification of the River Jordan, and sometimes accessories, such as the Raven who fed the Prophet (1 Kings xvii, 6), or the Children who mocked Elisha, and the Bears (2 Kings ii, 24). Above is the Hand of God issuing from a cloud.

Of the other passages in the Bible mentioning chariots, which are more historical than capable of symbolical interpretation, very few illustrations occur. Joseph in his chariot

---

[1] Sepulchral urn from Arles. (Martigny's *Dict.*, art. "*Mer Rouge*", p. 461.)

meeting his father Israel (Genesis xlvi, 29), is to be found on an ivory casket of the twelfth century at Sens in France,[1] and in the *Biblia Pauperum* Ahab is drawn in a chariot, with the dogs below ready to lick up his blood (1 Kings xxii, 35, 38). Chariots are described in Isaiah's vision of the destruction of Babylon (Isaiah xxi, 7-9), but I have never seen the text illustrated. In the representations of Sol and Luna in Christian art chariots occur, but they are, of course, borrowed from classical sources. In Adamnan's *Life of St. Columba* (chap. xliv) the Latin word *currus*, or chariot, is used to describe the vehicle in which the saint made his journeys.

Fig. 79.—The Baptism of Christ, with the two rivers Jor and Dan uniting in one Jordan, on the broken cross-shaft in Kells Churchyard.

There is an ancient Irish poem called the "Demoniac Chariot of Cu Chulaind" (see *Jour. R. H. and Archæol. Assoc. of Ireland*, vol. i, 4th Series, p, 371).

The fragments in the churchyard at Kells consist of part of the head of a cross lying on the ground, the broken shaft belonging to it being now erected on the old base. The head has the Crucifixion upon it, and the base is plain. The shaft, which measures 8 ft. 9 ins. high, and 2 ft. 6 ins wide, by 1 ft. 6 ins. thick, has upon it the following sculptures. On the front six panels, the lowest representing the Baptism of Christ, the others

---

[1] Viollet-le-Duc, *Dict. du Mobilier*, vol. i, p. 80. This scene is also illustrated in Ælfric's Heptateuch in the British Museum (Claud. B. iv).

difficult to identify. On the back five panels—(1) the Temptation of Adam and Eve; (2) Noah's Ark; (3) greatly defaced; (4) a fish with three kneeling figures on one side and four on the other. The sides are ornamented with spiral patterns and interlaced work. We have already discussed all the subjects found on this shaft with the exception of the Baptism of Christ, discussed in the next lecture, and Noah's Ark, of which this is, as far as I am aware, the only representation in Celtic art on stone or in illuminated MSS. The sculpture shows a vessel with high prows, having four windows or port-holes, and the dove perched on the top. The Ark of Noah has been used

Fig. 80.—Noah's Ark, on the broken cross-shaft in Kells Churchyard.

for purposes of symbolism from the time when the earliest paintings in the Catacombs were executed, and it has always been looked upon as a type of the Church, by entering which Christians may be saved from the spiritual destruction that overwhelms those without. The dove bearing the olive-branch signifies the peaceful rest awaiting the soul when the struggle with the world is over. We have ample evidence of the Scriptural origin of the symbol of the Ark. Ezekiel (xiv, 14) compares the delivery of Noah with that of Daniel; our Lord (Matt. xxiv, 37) likens the days of Noah to the coming of the Son of Man; St. Paul (Heb. xi, 7) tells us that Noah was saved by faith; and St. Peter (1 Pet. iii, 20) makes the saving of the Ark by water a figure of Baptism.

The earliest representations of Noah in the Ark in the paintings of the Catacombs and on the sculptured sarcophagi are of the most abstract possible character. The word ark is taken literally to mean a chest, and Noah is seen draped in a tunic, standing up in a square box, the lid of which is open, and provided in many cases with a hasp and lock.[1] His hands are either extended towards the dove, who is flying in the air with an olive-branch in its mouth, or raised in the ancient attitude of prayer. The meaning of the subject is made clear from examples inscribed NΩE on coins of Apamea in Phrygia, belonging to the reign of Septimius Severus[2] (in the third century). The town of Apamea assumed the name KIBΩTOΣ, or Ark, from its pretensions to be the place where the Ark had rested.[3] Noah in the Ark occurs less frequently on the sculptured sarcophagi than on the paintings in the Catacombs, and perhaps about the sixth century it disappears from art as an abstract symbol, and takes its place in the historical series illustrating the events in the Old Testament.

I only know of one instance of Noah's Ark in Norman sculpture, which occurs on the very remarkable slabs built into the west wall of Lincoln Cathedral.[4] An interesting early series of the Life of Noah is to be found on the ivory plaques in the Cathedral of Salerno, of which there are casts in the South Kensington Museum.[5]

Instead of a mere box containing the figure of a man, we have, from the eleventh century onwards. an elaborately drawn vessel supporting a house, with highly finished architectural details, from the windows of which Noah and his family and the various animals can be seen looking out. Saxon representations of this class are to be found in Ælfric's *Heptateuch* (Brit. Mus., Claud. B. iv), and in Cædmon's *Paraphrase of the Scriptures* in the Bodleian, and twelfth century examples in the Brit. Mus.

---

[1] In one case Noah is placed in a round tub with beasts' heads on it. (Garrucci, *Storia del Arte Cristiana*, vol. ii, pl. 72.)

[2] Martigny's *Dict.*, art. "*Numismatique Chrétienne*", p. 518.

[3] Northcote and Brownlow, *Roma Sotterranea*, vol. ii, p. 107.

[4] *Jour. Brit. Archæol. Inst.*, vol. xxv, p. 1.

[5] Westwood's *Catalogue of Fictile Ivories*, p. 63.

MSS. (Nero C. iv), and the Spanish Apocalypse (Add. MS. 11,695).[1]

The cross near the market-place of Kells is 11 ft. 6 ins. high (including the base, which is 2 ft. 6 ins. high), and measures 4 ft. across the arms. The top arm has been broken off, and one panel of sculpture at the bottom of the shaft is entirely effaced by an inscription cut in 1688. The subjects of the sculpture are: on the front, the Crucifixion in the centre of the head of the cross, with pairs of ecclesiastics holding croziers on each side, and a figure tumbling head downwards; below, on the shaft, three panels much defaced.[2] On the back, Daniel surrounded by four lions in the centre of the head of the cross, with a man between two figures having human bodies and beasts' heads on

Fig. 81.—One side of the base of the Cross in the town of Kells.

the right, and the Sacrifice of Isaac on the left. Below, on the shaft, three panels—(1) Temptation and Expulsion of Adam and Eve; (2) a gigantic warrior and several small figures; (3) soldiers watching the sepulchre of Christ. On the ends of the arms of the cross, two ecclesiastics with croziers placed crosswise, and bird holding circular object between them,[3] and David rending the Lion's Jaw. On the left side of the shaft four panels—(1) Man with horns between two beasts; (2) three men with legs and arms clasped together; (3) two figures

[1] Also see Spanish Apocalypse belonging to Messrs. Firmin Didot, of Paris, illustrated in Paul Lacroix, *Literature and Science of the Middle Ages*, p. 111.

[2] The top one appears to have upon it a seated figure, holding in his right hand five circular discs and in his left a pair of fish crossed, possibly symbolising the miracle of the Loaves and Fishes.

[3] As on cross of SS. Patrick and Columba at Kells.

defaced ; (4) two men wrestling. On the right side four panels—
(1) Hand symbol and three figures; (2) male and female figure;
(3) man placed head downwards with figure at each side; (4)
stag and man. On the four sides of the base—(1) Two centaurs,
three birds, fish, and two animals; (2) five warriors with spears,
shields, and swords, fighting; (3) man, bird, two stags, and five
other animals; (4) four warriors on horseback.

In concluding our review of the symbolism of the Irish
crosses, it must be observed that, although we have been able
to explain the subjects which occur most frequently, there is
still much which, in the present state of our knowledge, we
cannot expect to understand, and it is not until more workers
enter this field of research that further progress can be made.
At present we only see as in a glass darkly, but the glimpses we
get through the dim mists of past ages are enough to stimulate
our curiosity to the utmost, and make us hope that the veil
will some day be raised which now obscures our view.

GENERAL INDEX.

INDEX OF SUBJECTS OCCURRING IN CHRISTIAN ART.

Note.— The numbers marked with an asterisk show the page on which the subject is specially described in detail.

LIST OF ILLUSTRATIONS.